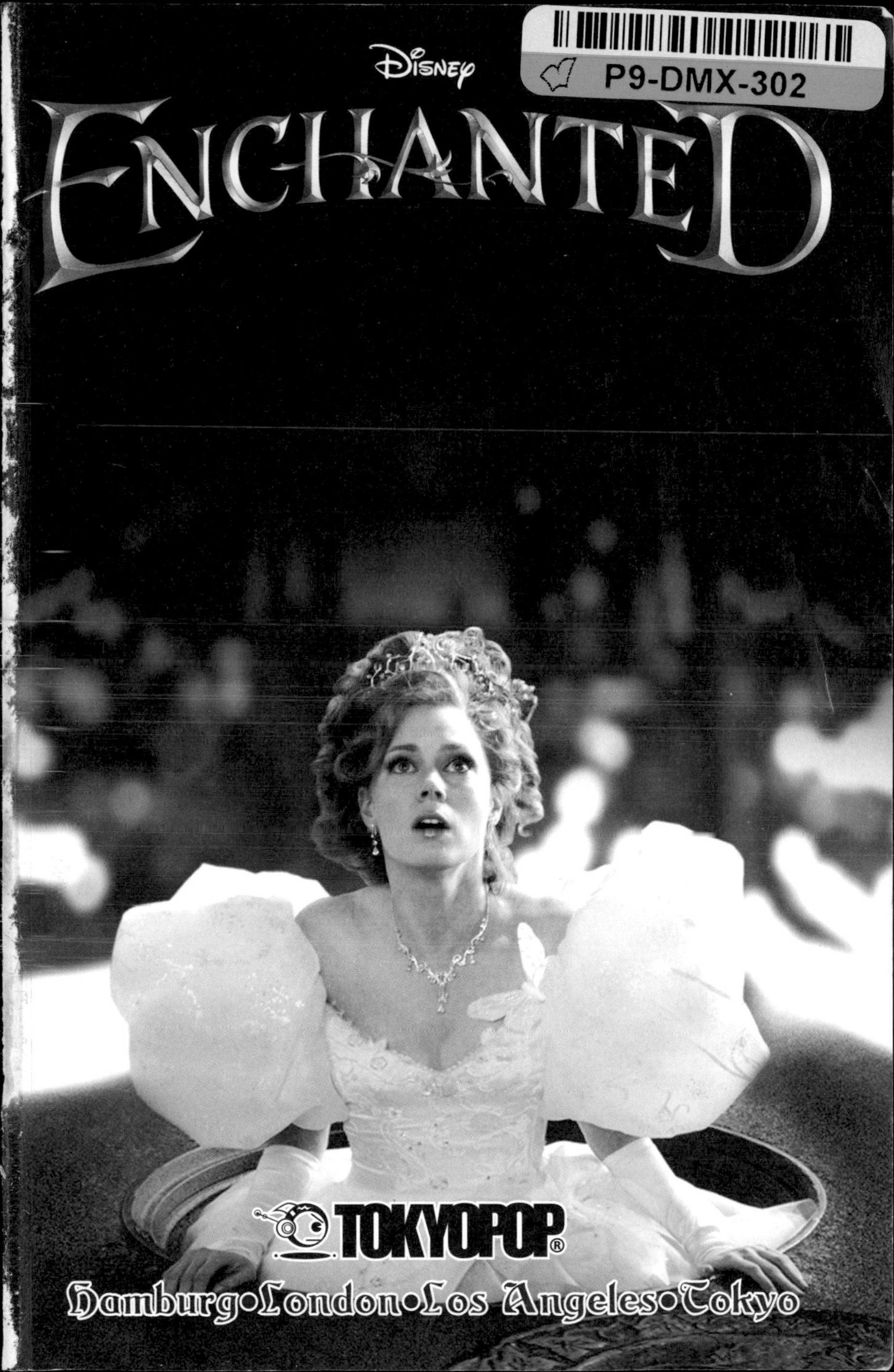
Disney
ENCHANTED
TOKYOPOP®
Hamburg•London•Los Angeles•Tokyo

Editor - Julie Taylor
Contributing Editor - Zachary Rau
Graphic Designer and Letterer - Lindsay Seligman
Cover Designer - Lindsay Seligman & Monalisa J. de Asis
Graphic Artist - Monalisa J. de Asis

Production Manager - Elisabeth Brizzi
Art Director - Anne Marie Horne
Editor in Chief - Rob Tokar
Publisher - Mike Kiley
President & C.O.O. - John Parker
C.E.O. & Chief Creative Officer - Stuart Levy

E-mail: info@TOKYOPOP.com
Come visit us online at www.TOKYOPOP.com

A **TOKYOPOP** Cine-Manga® Book
TOKYOPOP Inc.
5900 Wilshire Blvd., Suite 2000
Los Angeles, CA 90036

Enchanted
Adapted by Renee Tawa and Susan Greager Cawman
Based on the screenplay written by Bill Kelly
Executive Producers Chris Chase, Sunil Perkash, Ezra Swerdlow
Produced by Barry Josephson and Barry Sonnenfeld
Directed by Kevin Lima

ISBN: 978-1-4278-0361-0

First TOKYOPOP® printing: December 2007

10 9 8 7 6 5 4 3 2 1

Printed in the United States

Table of Contents

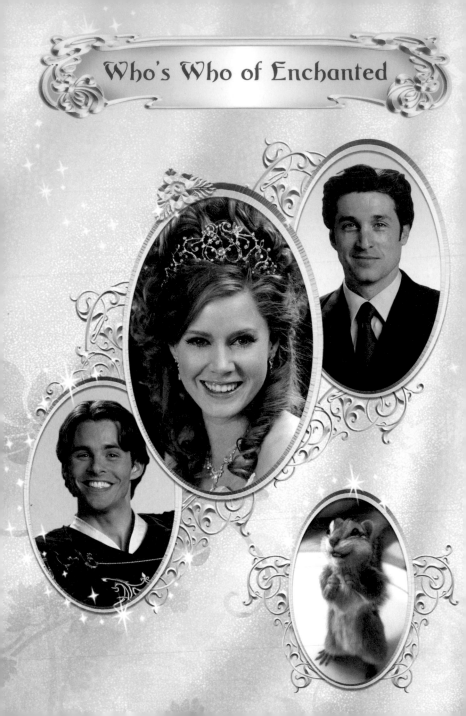

Who's Who of Enchanted

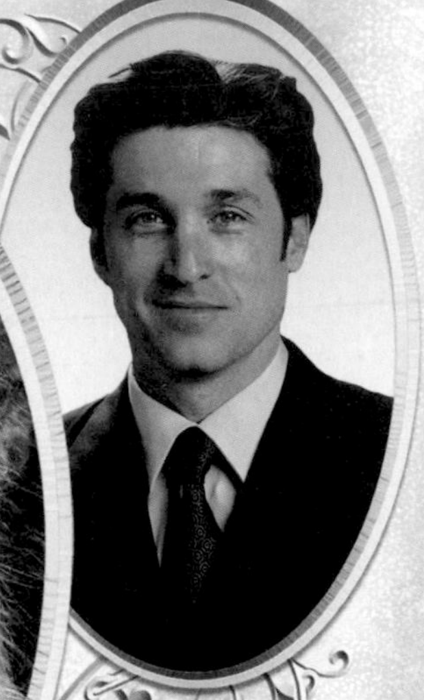

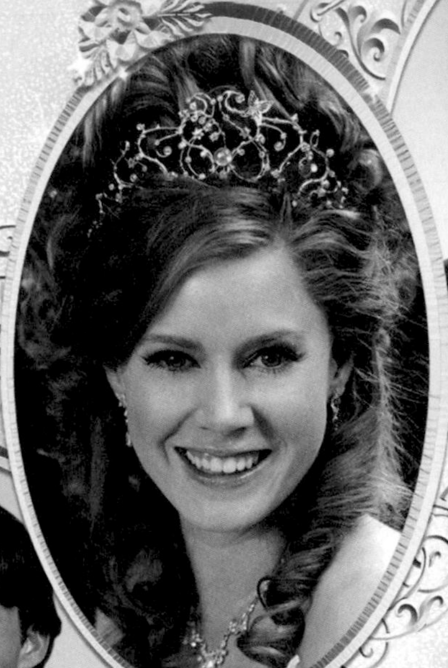

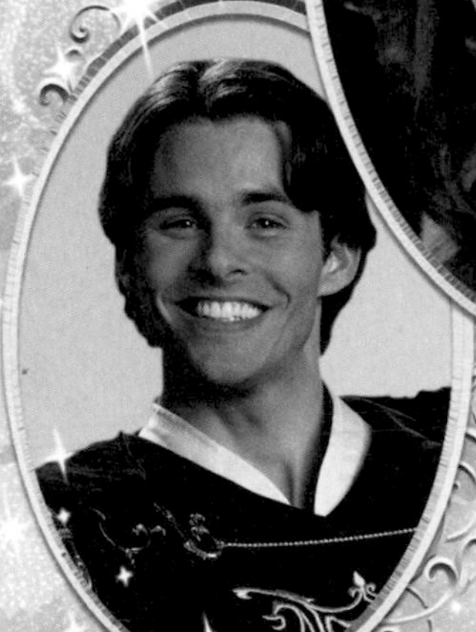

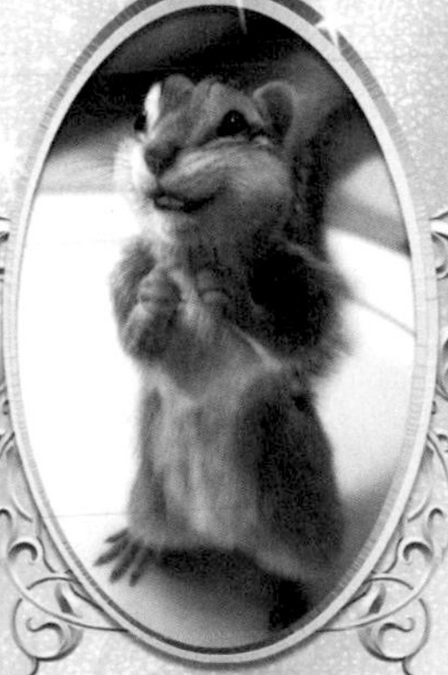

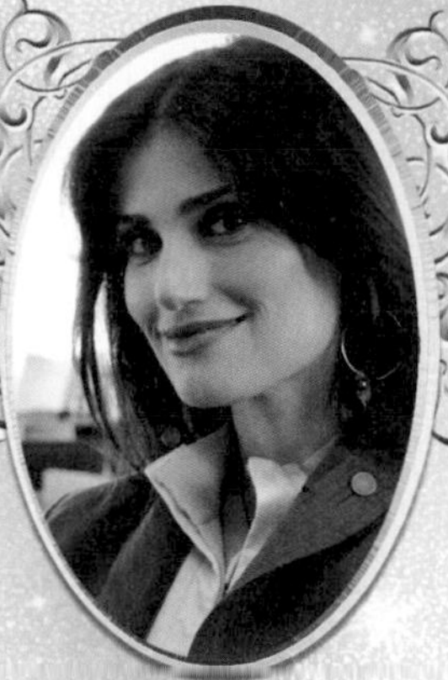
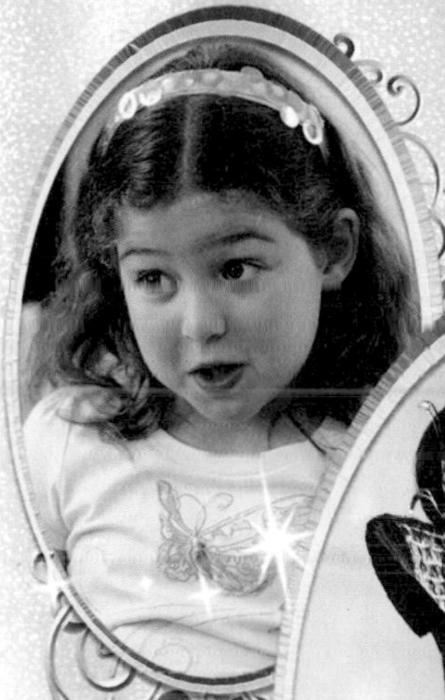
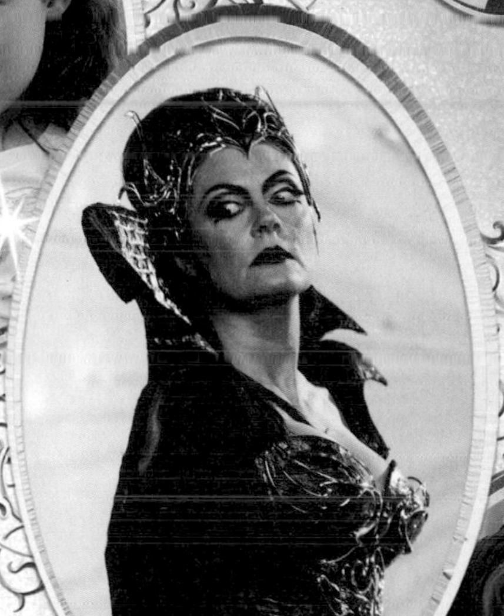
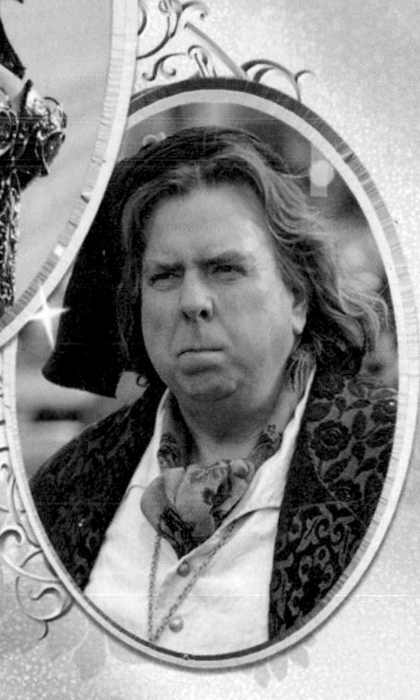

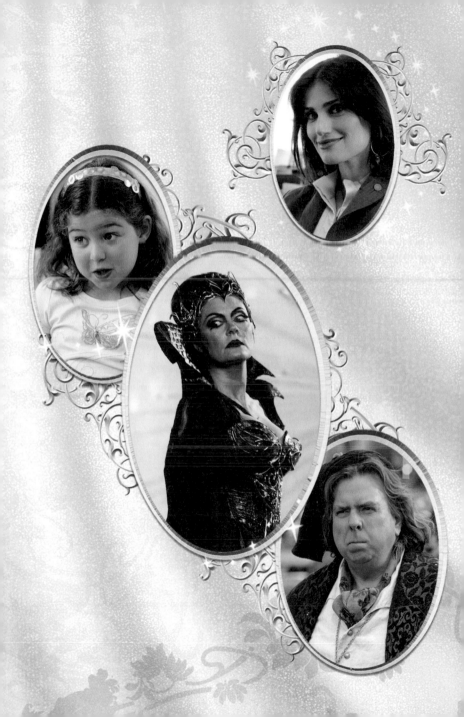

Giselle

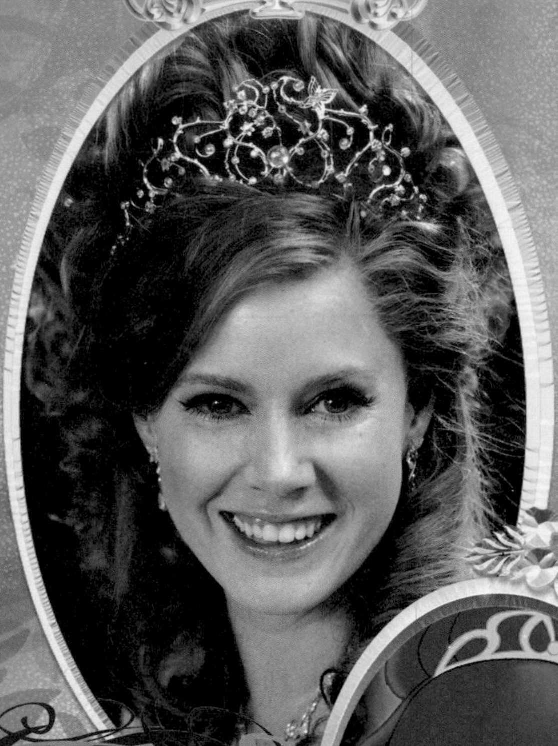

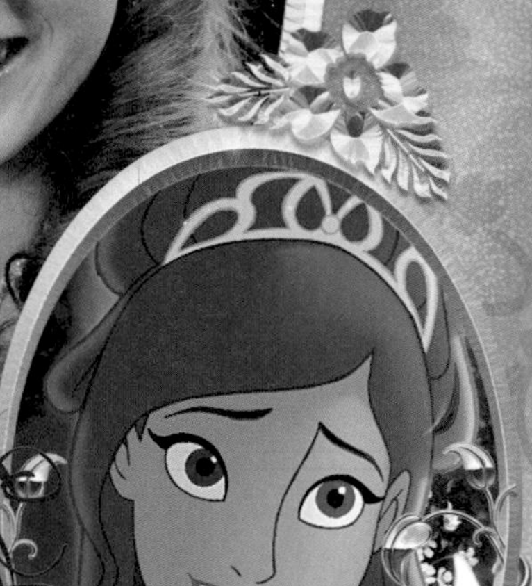

A lonely princess who dreams of finding her prince and living happily ever after.

Robert

A handsome divorce
attorney who loves his
daughter, Morgan. They
live in New York City.

Morgan

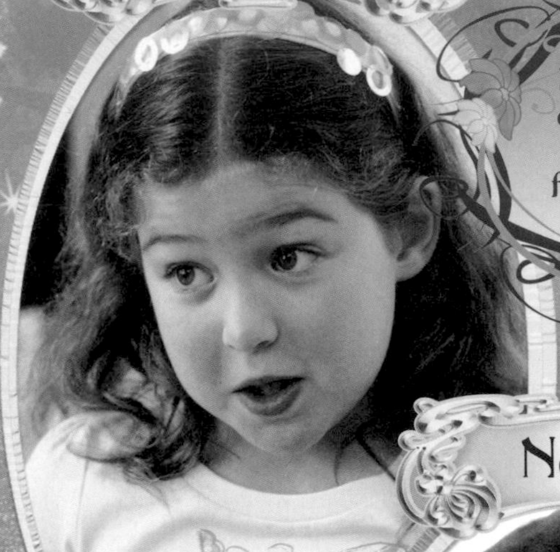

Morgan is Robert's only child. Her mom left her and her father when she was still a baby.

Nancy

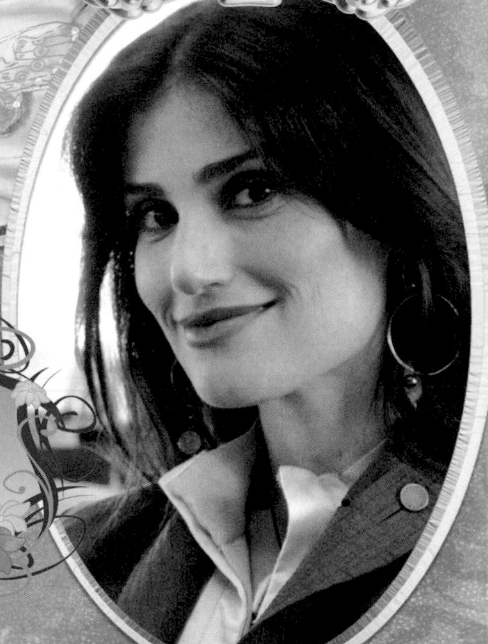

Nancy is Robert's girlfriend, though she is not well-liked by Morgan.

Prince Edward

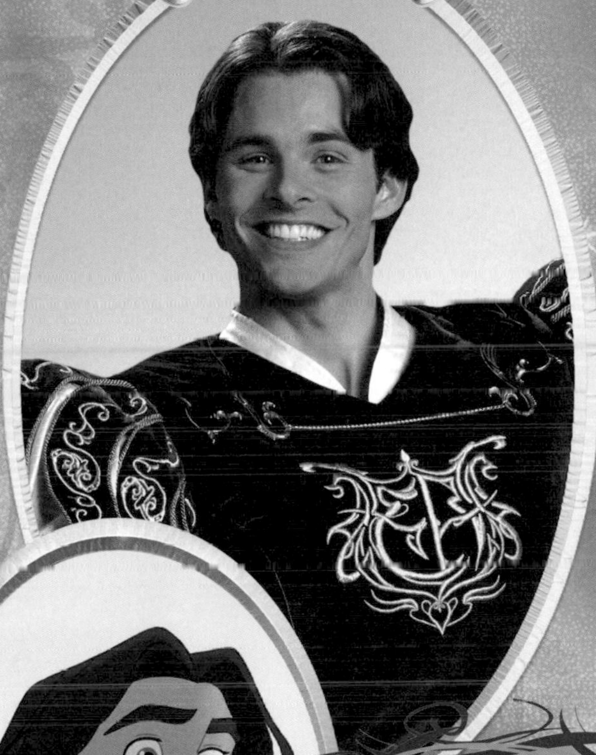

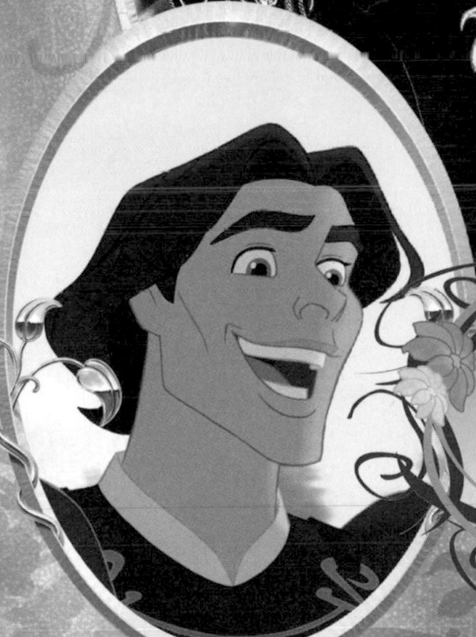

He is the step-son of Queen Narissa and the Prince of Andalasia, but not necessarily the brightest man in the kingdom.

Pip

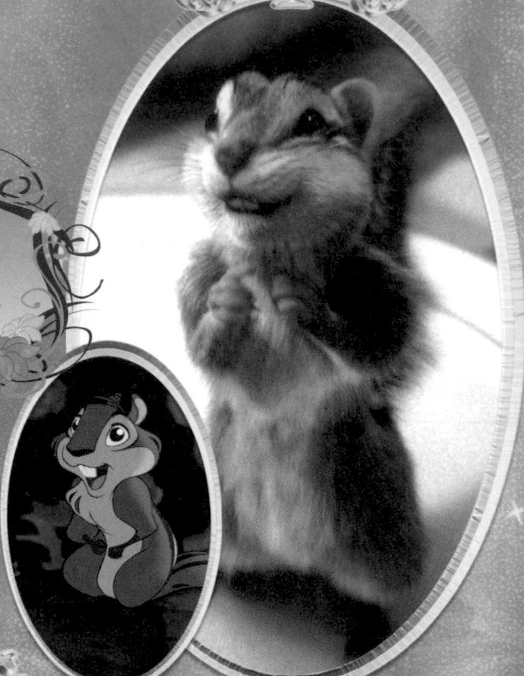

Pip is Giselle's best friend and sidekick in Andalasia.

Nathaniel

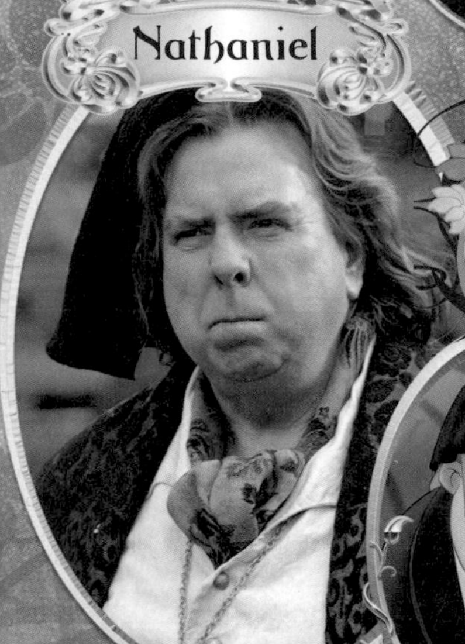

Nathaniel claims to be the prince's friend but secretly performs evil deeds for the queen, whom he loves.

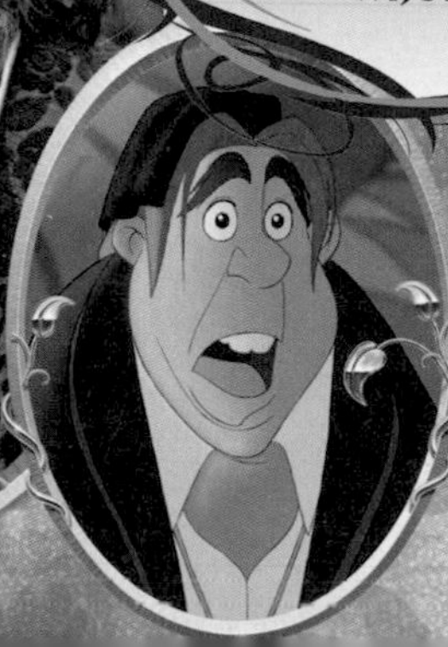

Queen Narissa

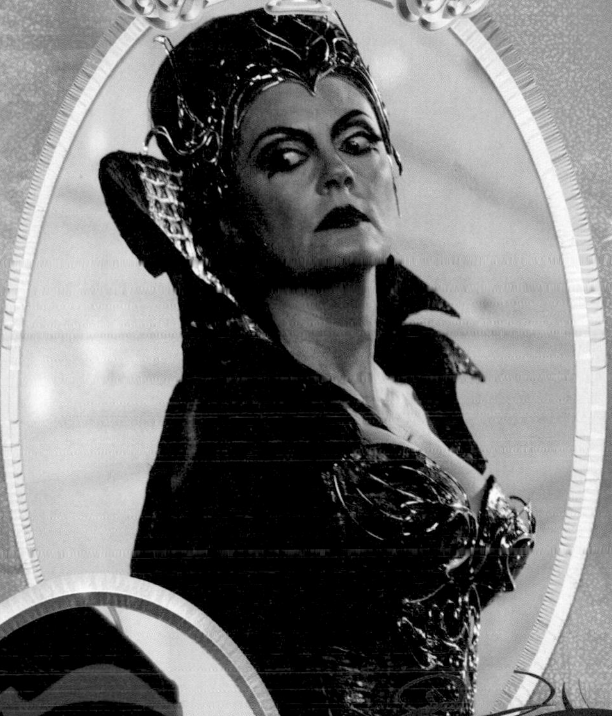

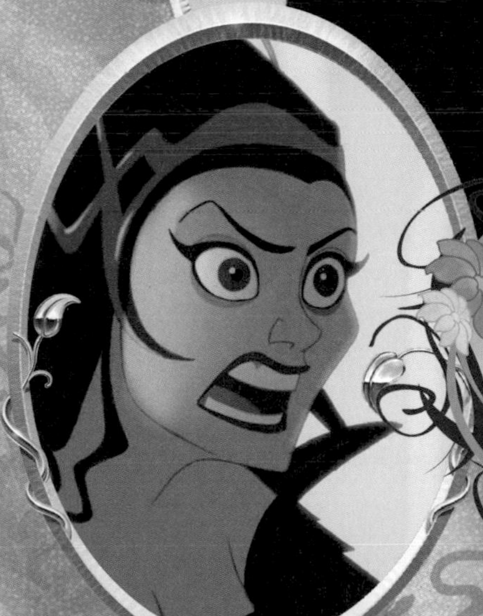

Queen Narissa is queen of Andalasia and step-mother to Prince Edward. She is an evil and deceitful queen who loves power more than anything else.

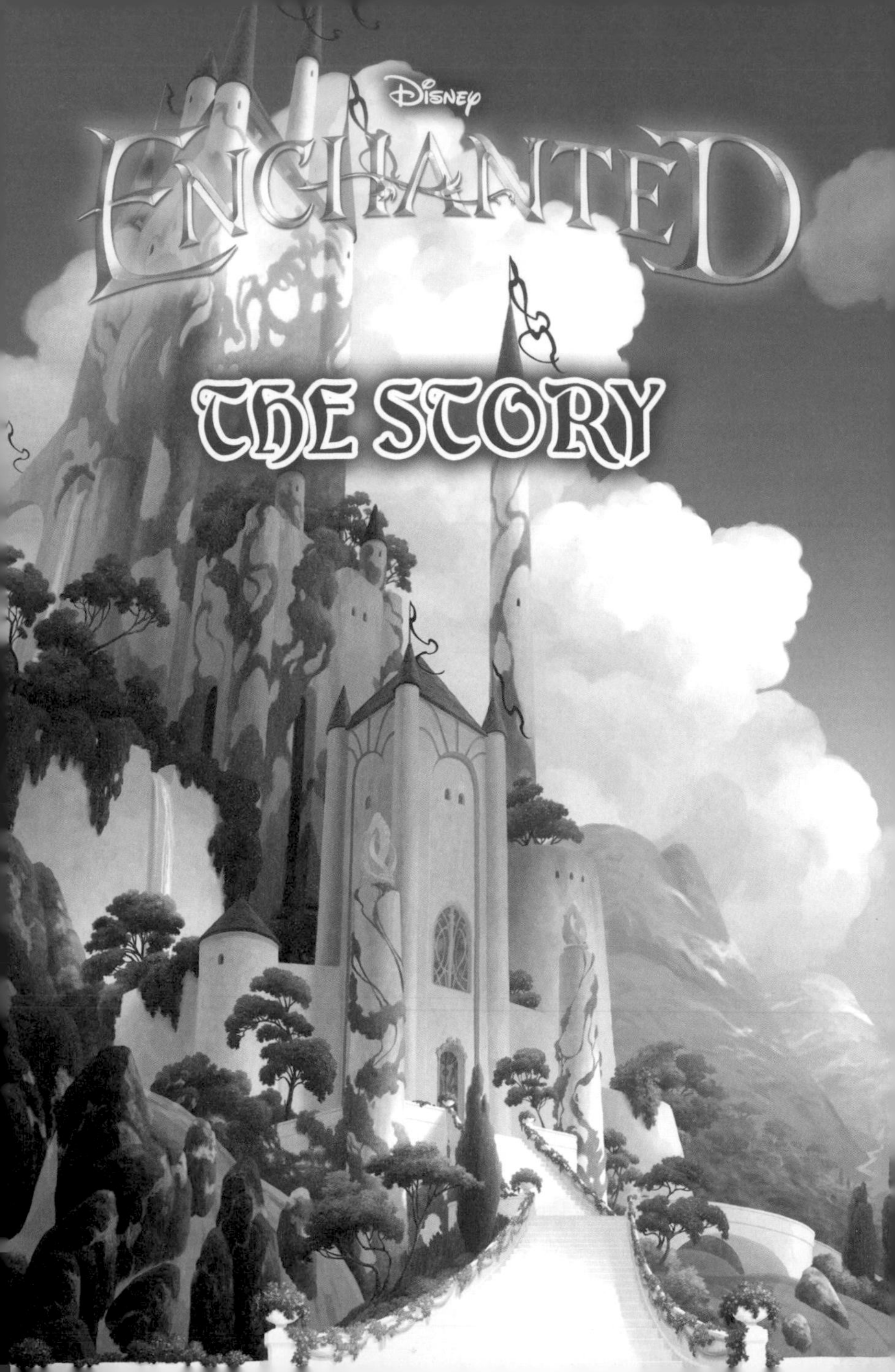
Disney
Enchanted
The Story

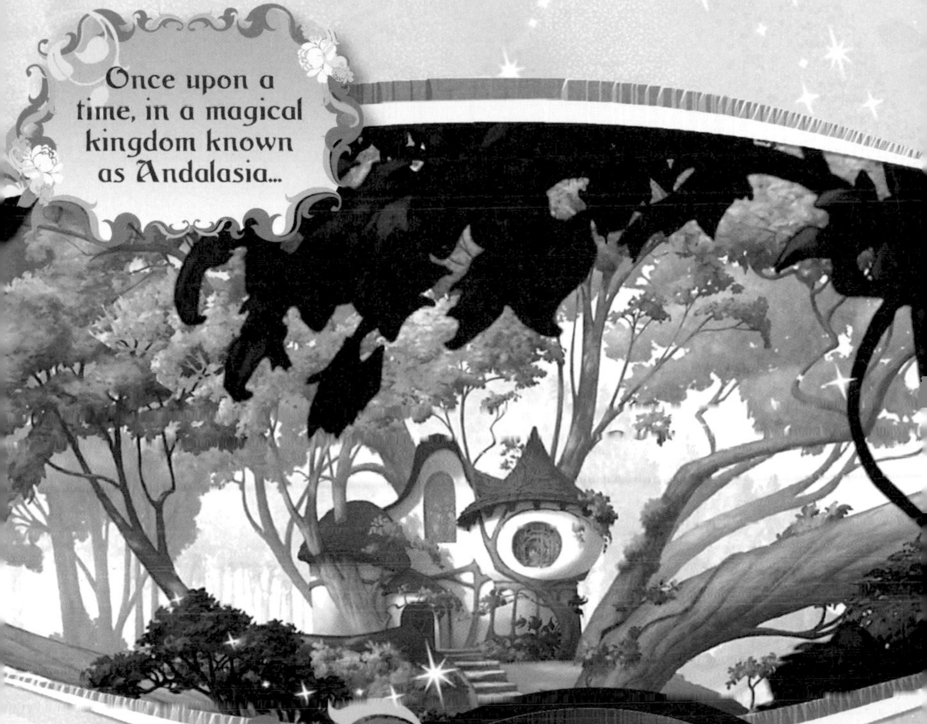
Once upon a time, in a magical kingdom known as Andalasia...

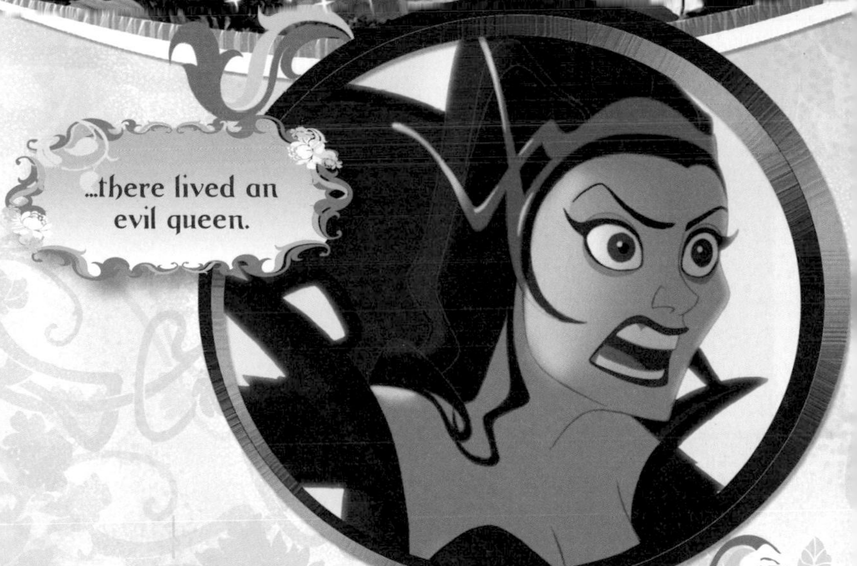
...there lived an evil queen.

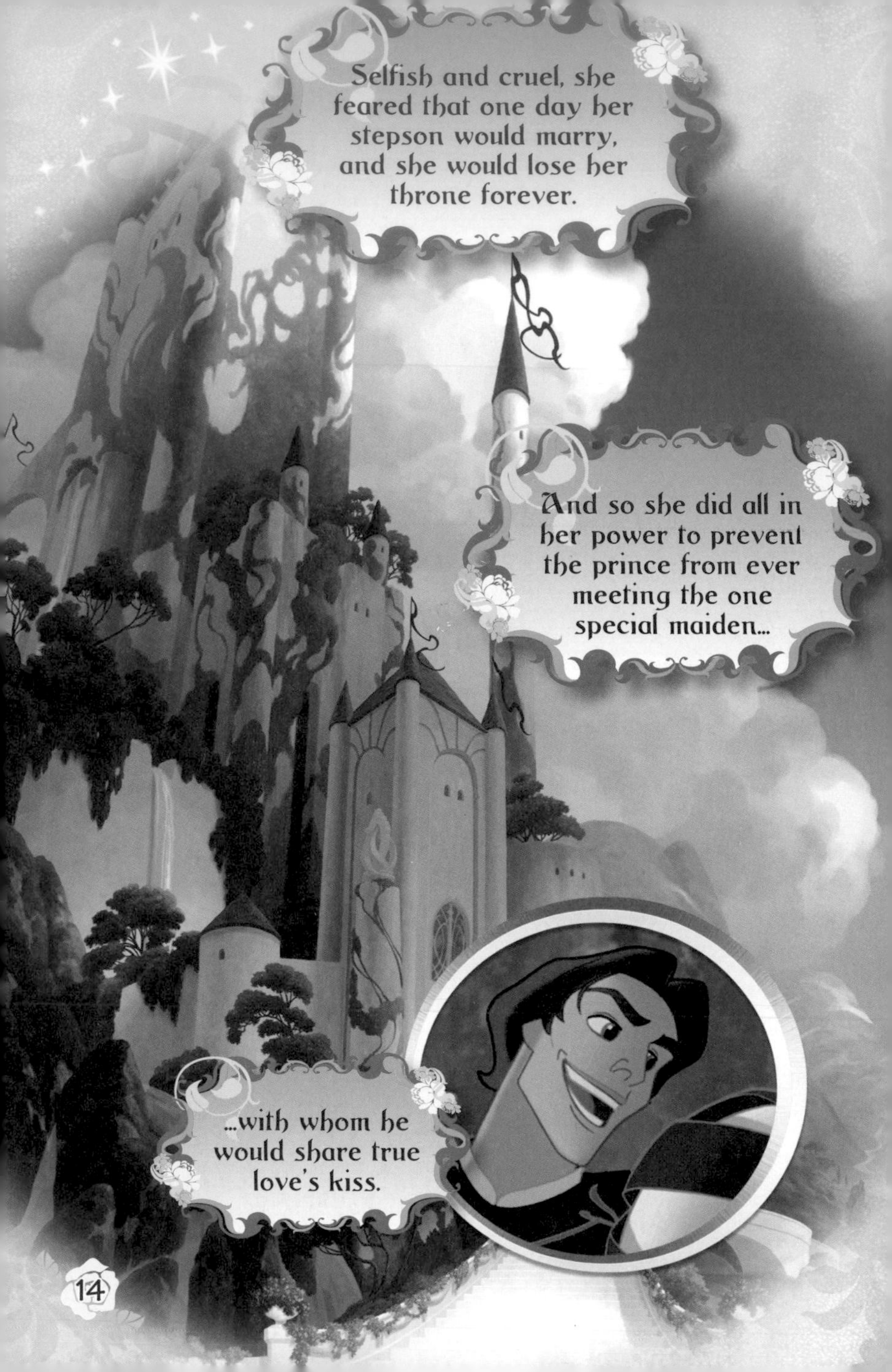
Selfish and cruel, she feared that one day her stepson would marry, and she would lose her throne forever.
And so she did all in her power to prevent the prince from ever meeting the one special maiden...
...with whom he would share true love's kiss.

Somewhere in Andalasia...
Okay ya mokes, move it! We gotta face ta put together here, while it's still ingrained in her subcranium!
Oh Pip, it was such a lovely dream. We were holding hands and dancing and...
And these for the eyes!
Blue! Oh, how did you know?! And they sparkle just like his! There we go. Yes, that's it!
Okay!
Floor's yours, honey.

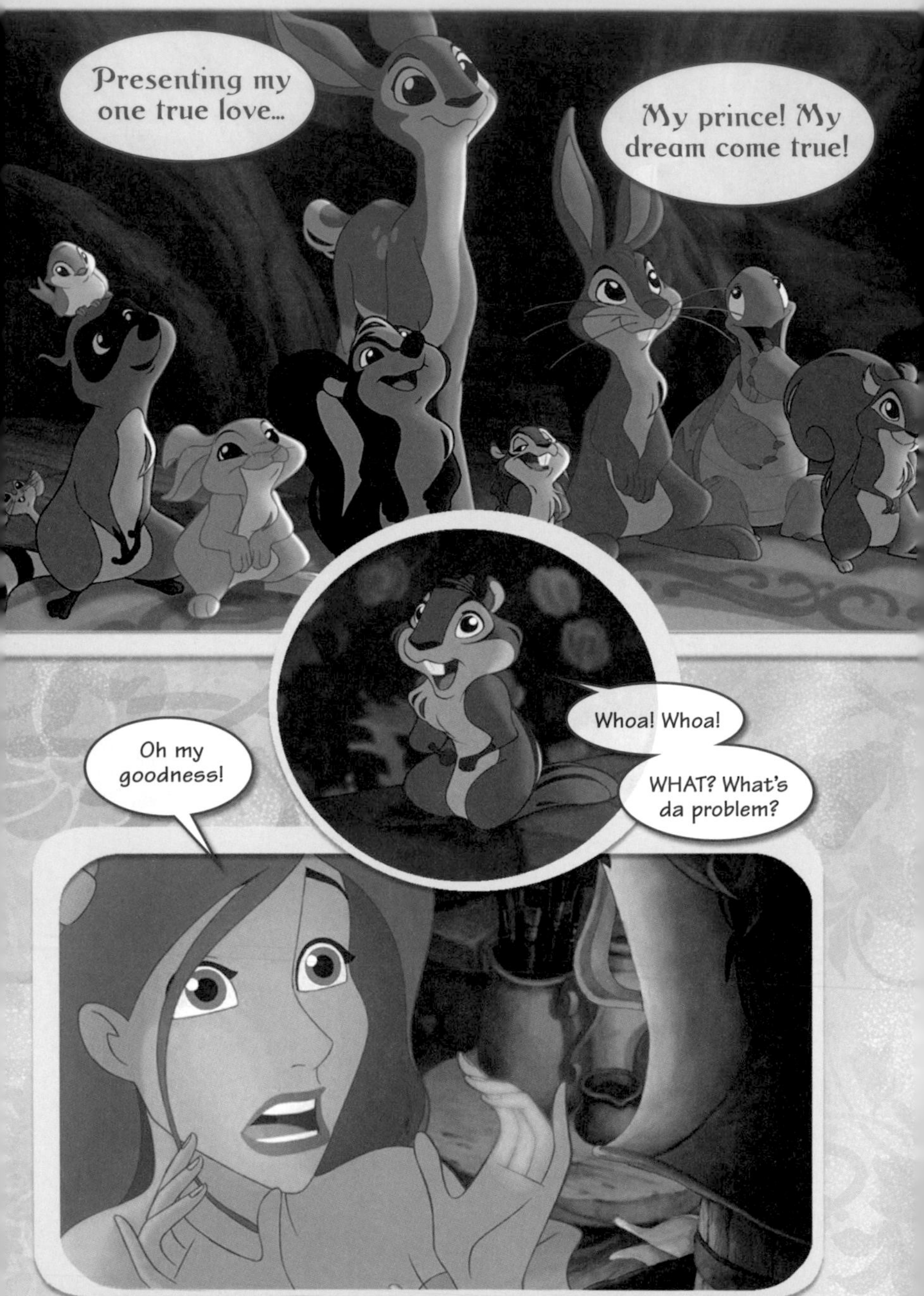
Presenting my one true love...
My prince! My dream come true!
Oh my goodness!
Whoa! Whoa!
WHAT? What's da problem?

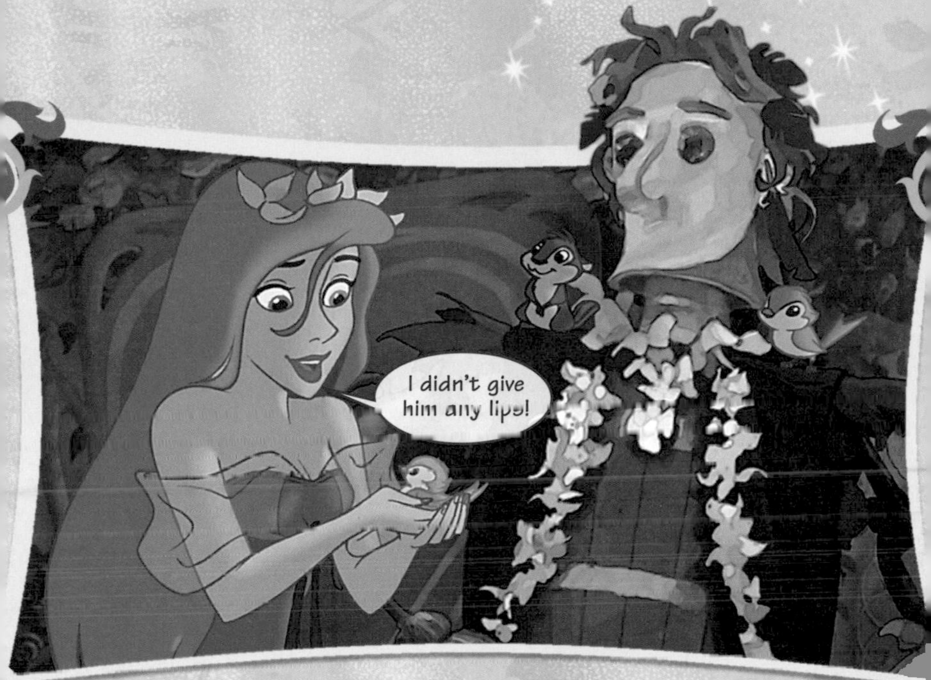
I didn't give him any lips!

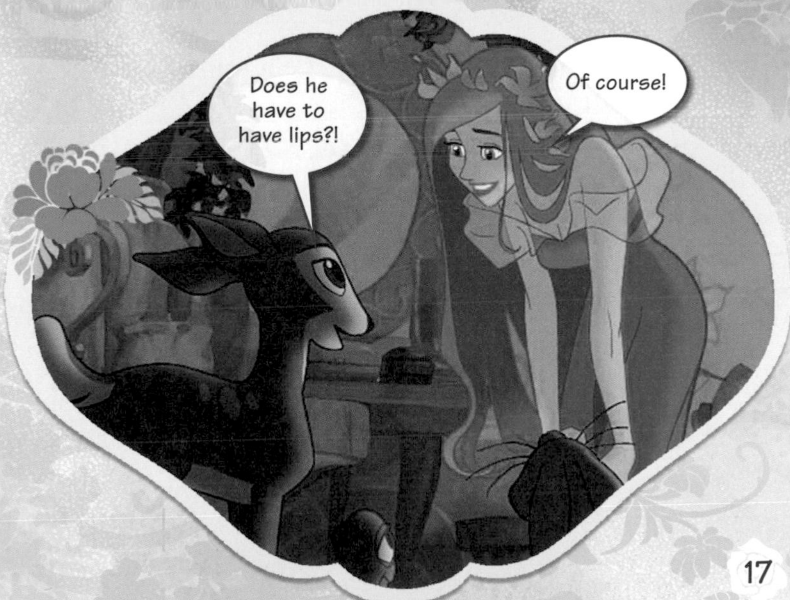
Does he have to have lips?!
Of course!

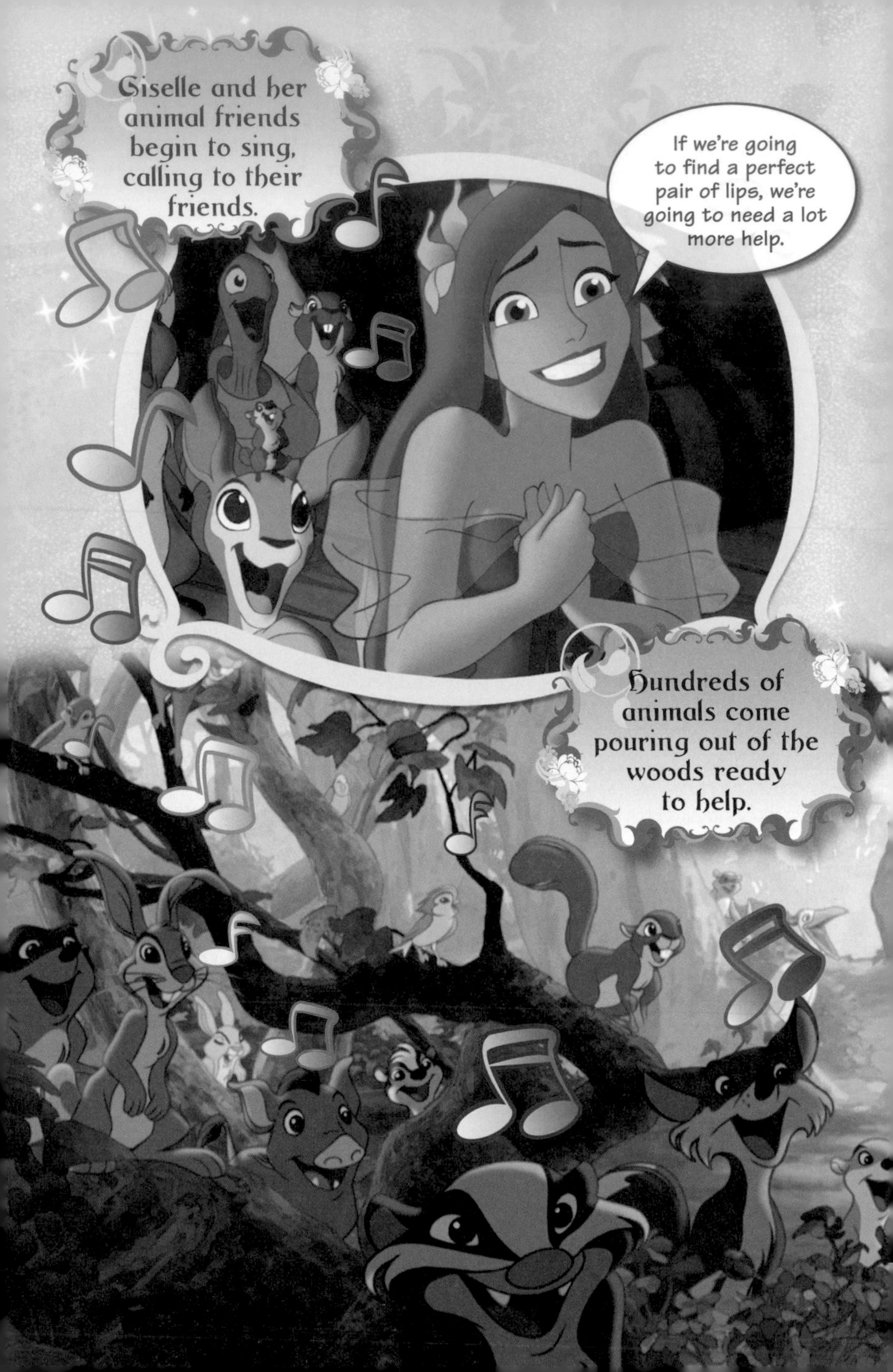
Giselle and her animal friends begin to sing, calling to their friends.
If we're going to find a perfect pair of lips, we're going to need a lot more help.
Hundreds of animals come pouring out of the woods ready to help.

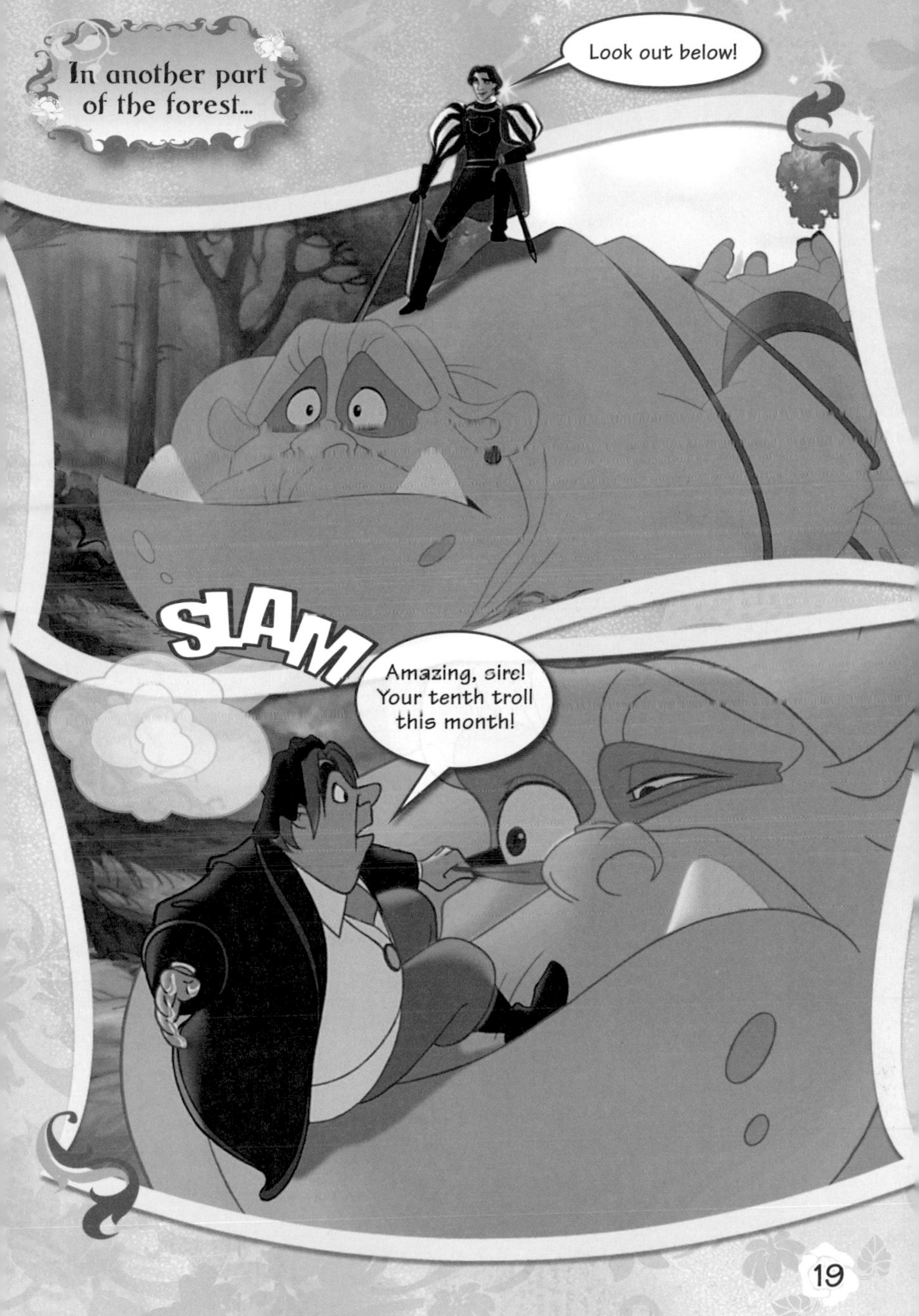
In another part of the forest...
Look out below!
SLAM
Amazing, sire! Your tenth troll this month!

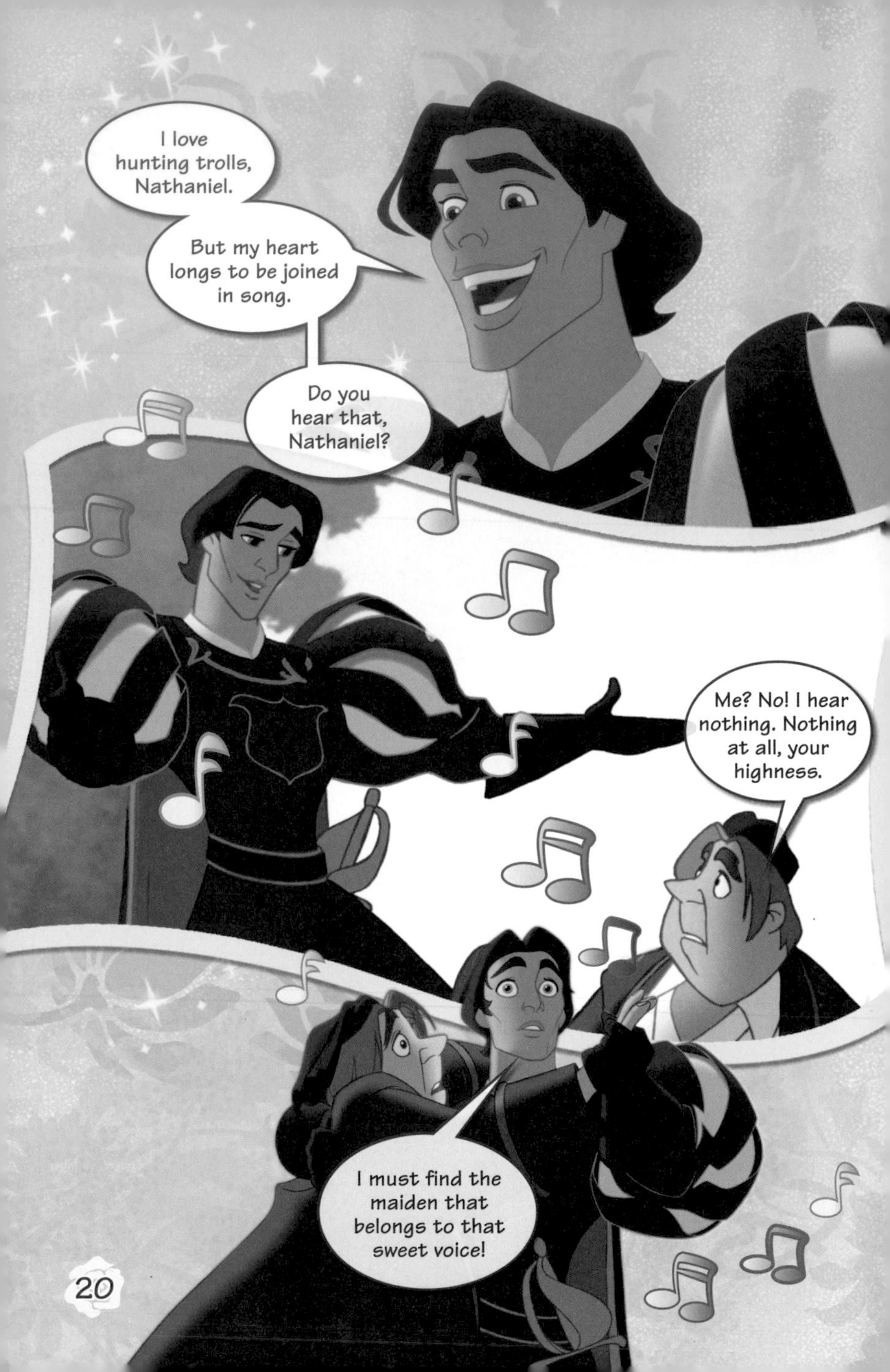
I love hunting trolls, Nathaniel.
But my heart longs to be joined in song.
Do you hear that, Nathaniel?
Me? No! I hear nothing. Nothing at all, your highness.
I must find the maiden that belongs to that sweet voice!

The prince jumps on his trusted steed...
Oh no! Come back, sire!
Ride, Destiny!
Oh poo! This isn't good! All these years of troll chasing and trying to keep him from ever meeting a girl! Oh, the queen... she's not going to like this!!!
...and races toward the angelic voice.
That maiden is mine!

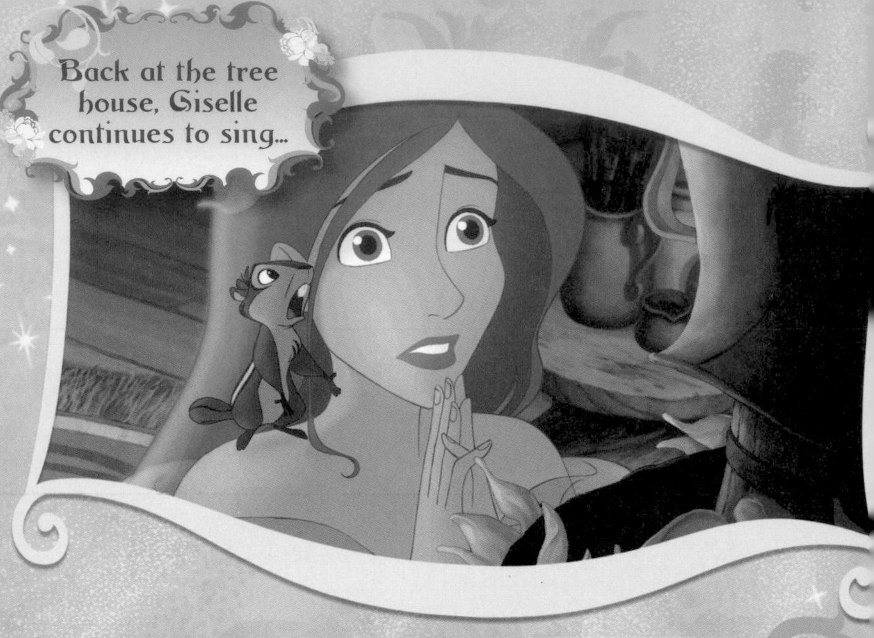
Back at the tree house, Giselle continues to sing...

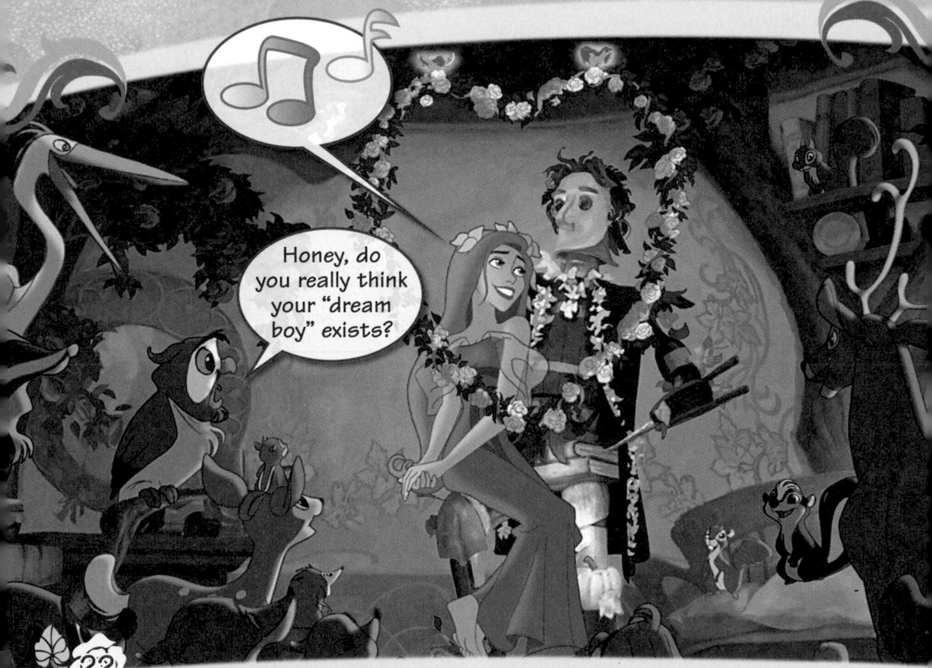
Honey, do you really think your "dream boy" exists?

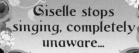

Giselle stops singing, completely unaware...

Oh Pip...

...I know he's out there somewhere!

...that her beautiful voice has led a troll directly to her.

HUH?

Eye, eye, eye.

I...I...what?

I eat you now!

23

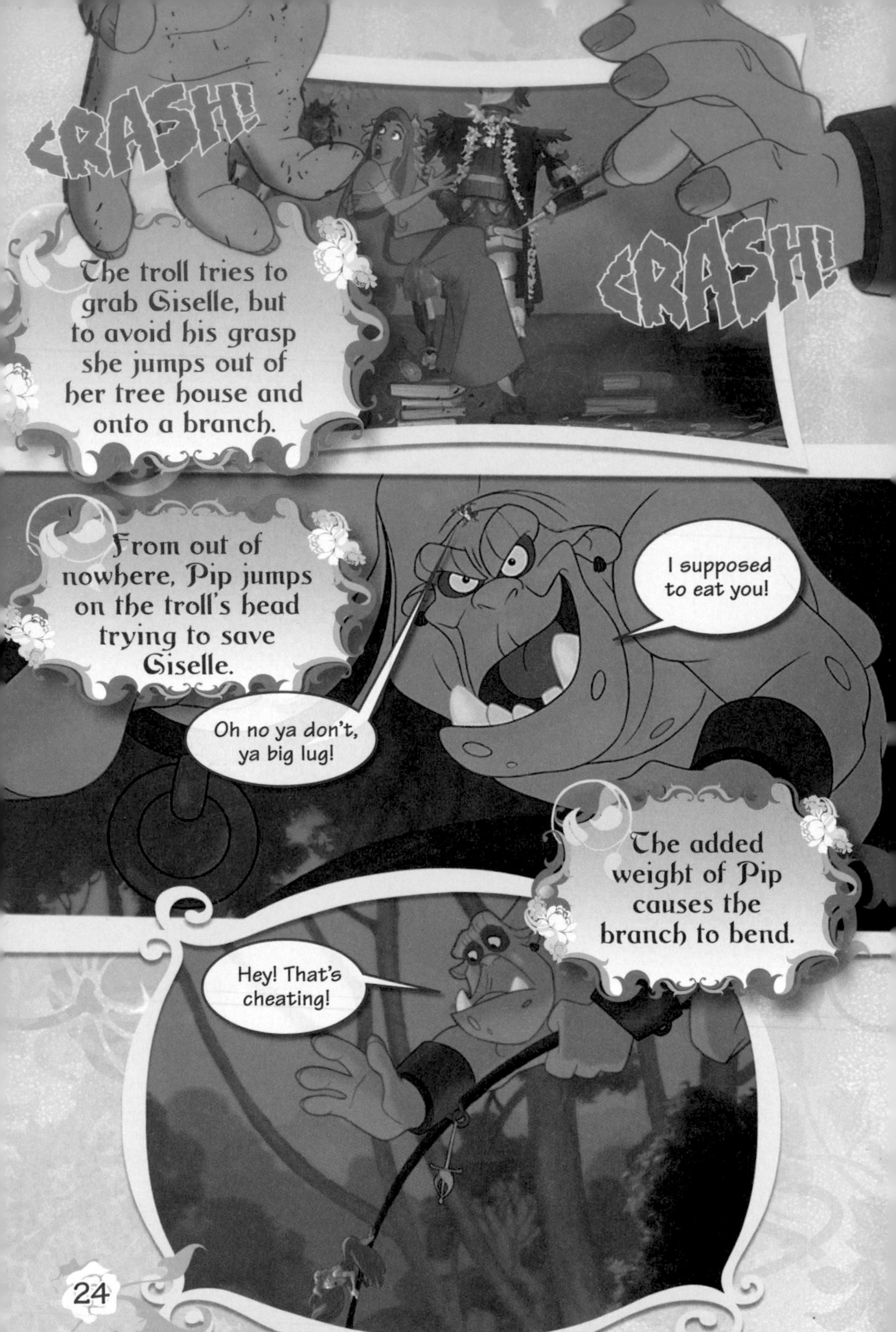
CRASH!
The troll tries to grab Giselle, but to avoid his grasp she jumps out of her tree house and onto a branch.
CRASH!
From out of nowhere, Pip jumps on the troll's head trying to save Giselle.
I supposed to eat you!
Oh no ya don't, ya big lug!
The added weight of Pip causes the branch to bend.
Hey! That's cheating!

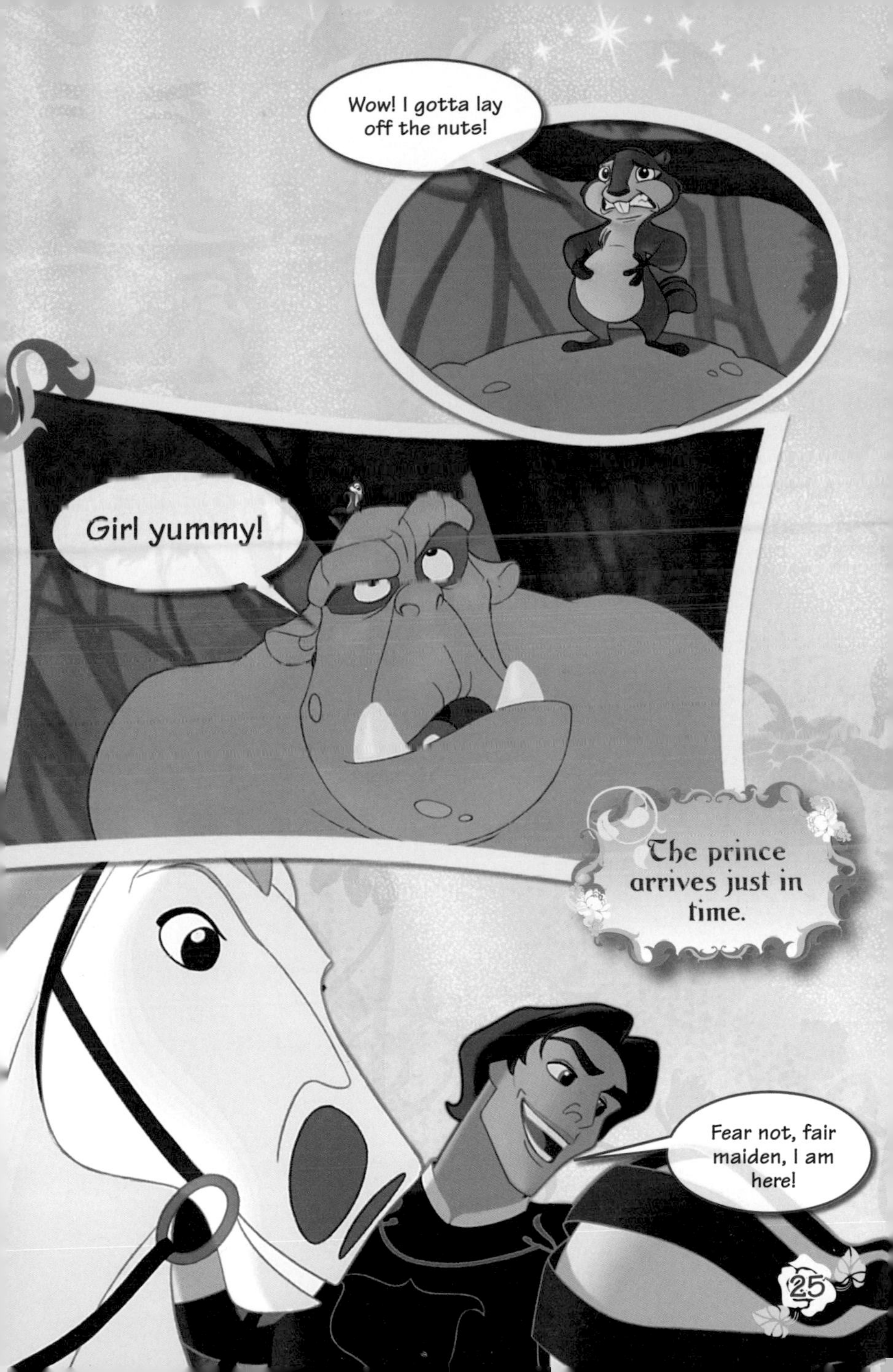
Wow! I gotta lay off the nuts!
Girl yummy!
The prince arrives just in time.
Fear not, fair maiden, I am here!

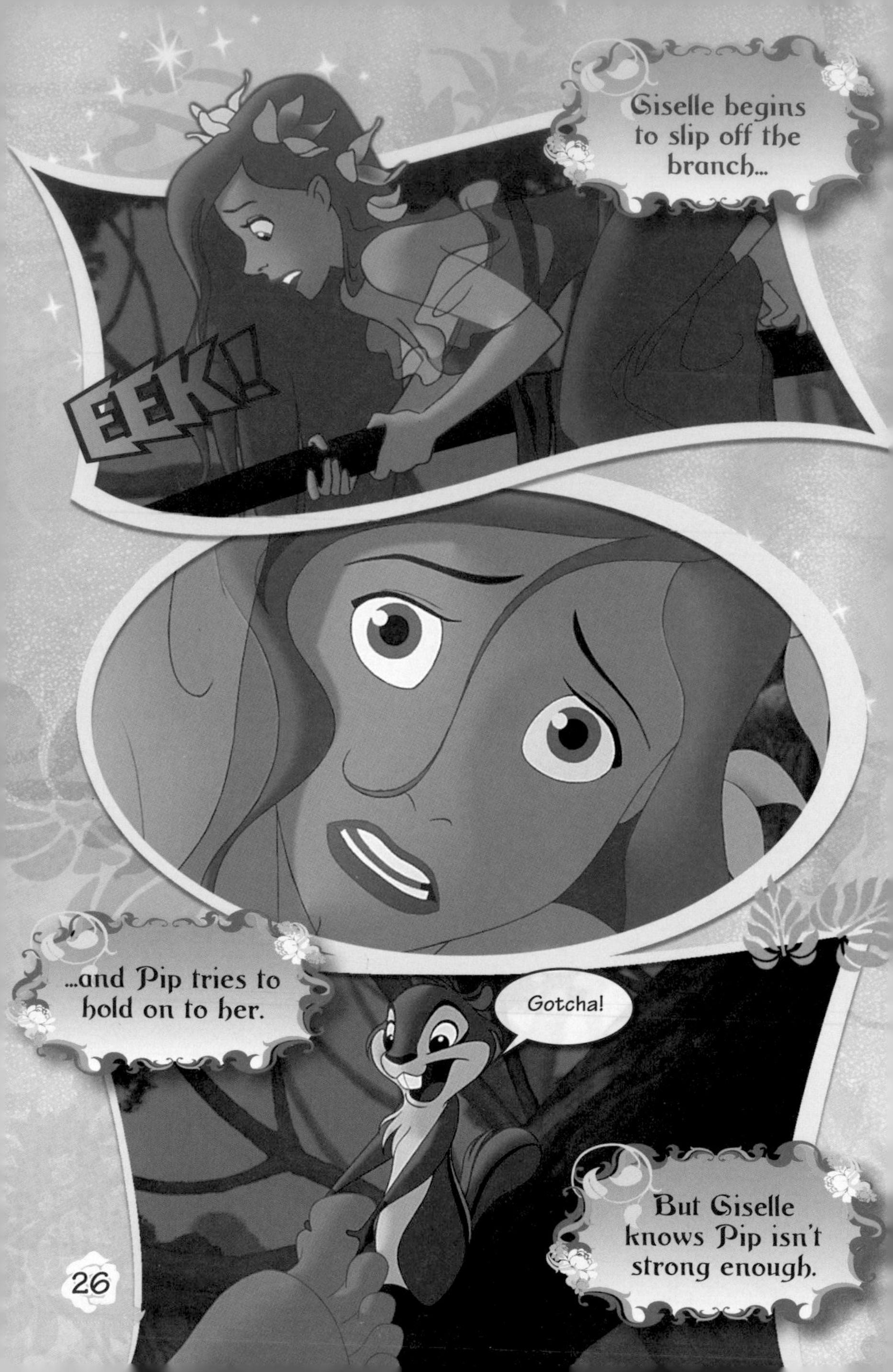
Giselle begins to slip off the branch...
EEK!
...and Pip tries to hold on to her.
Gotcha!
But Giselle knows Pip isn't strong enough.

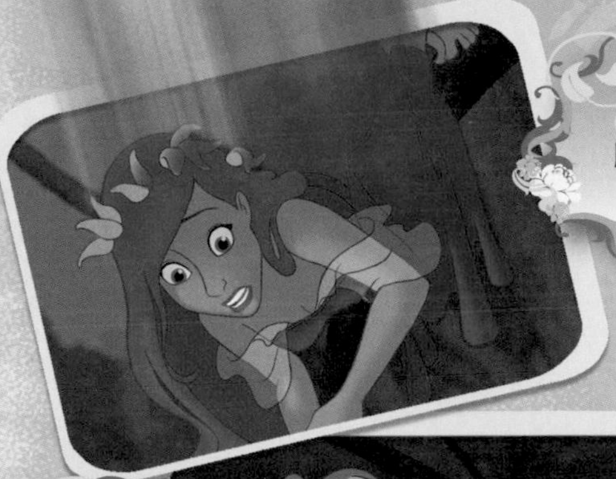
Giselle looses her grip on the branch...

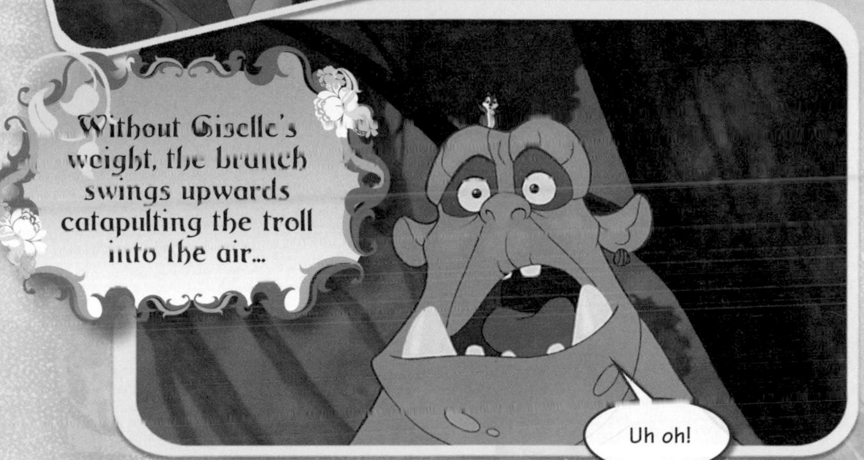
Without Giselle's weight, the branch swings upwards catapulting the troll into the air...
Uh oh!

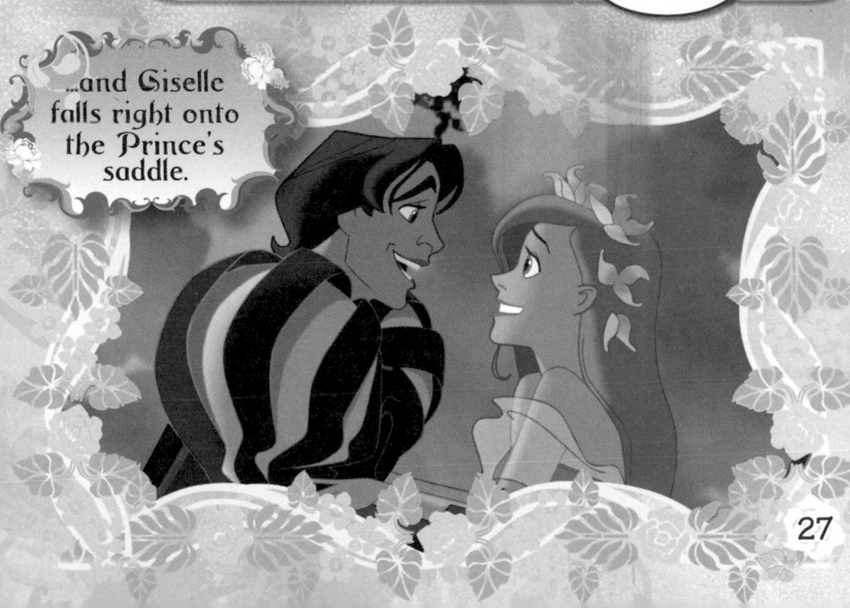
...and Giselle falls right onto the Prince's saddle.

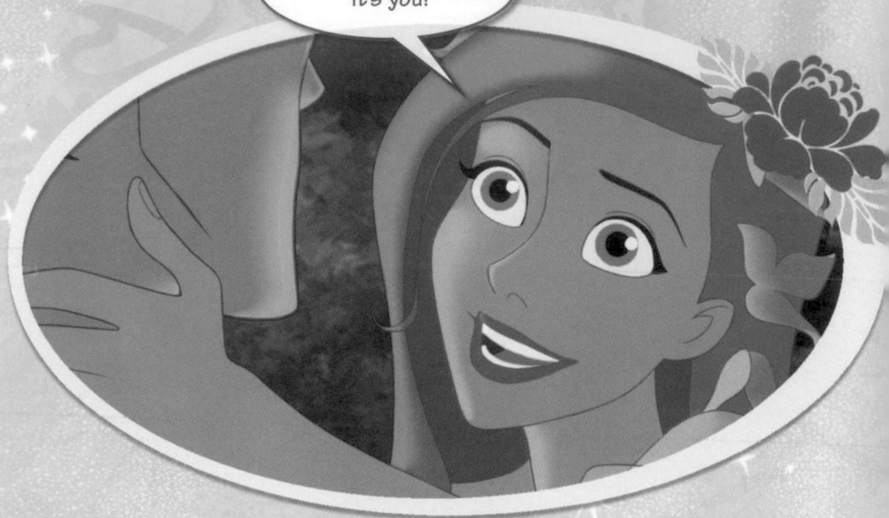
Oh my gosh!
It's you!

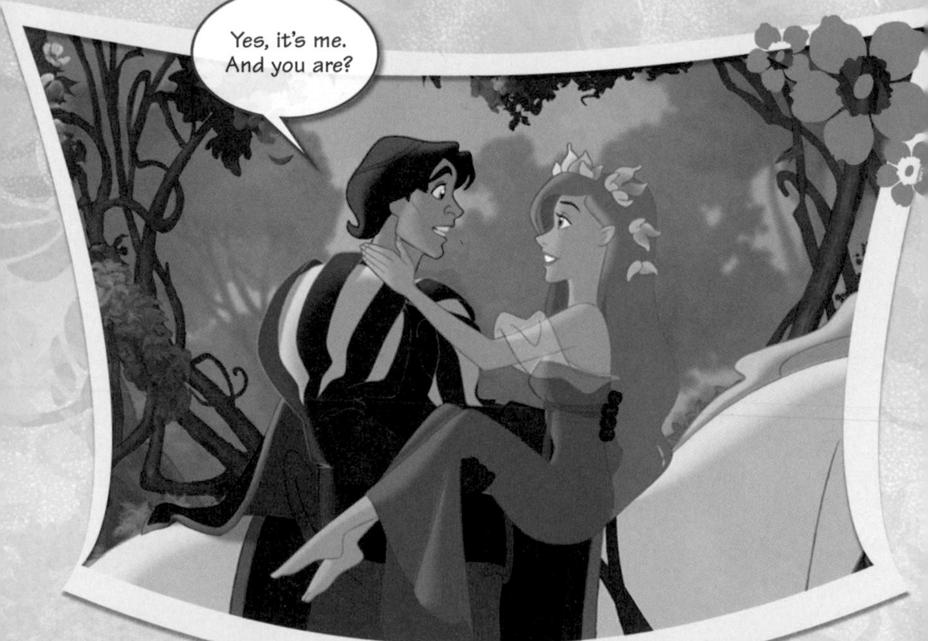
Yes, it's me.
And you are?

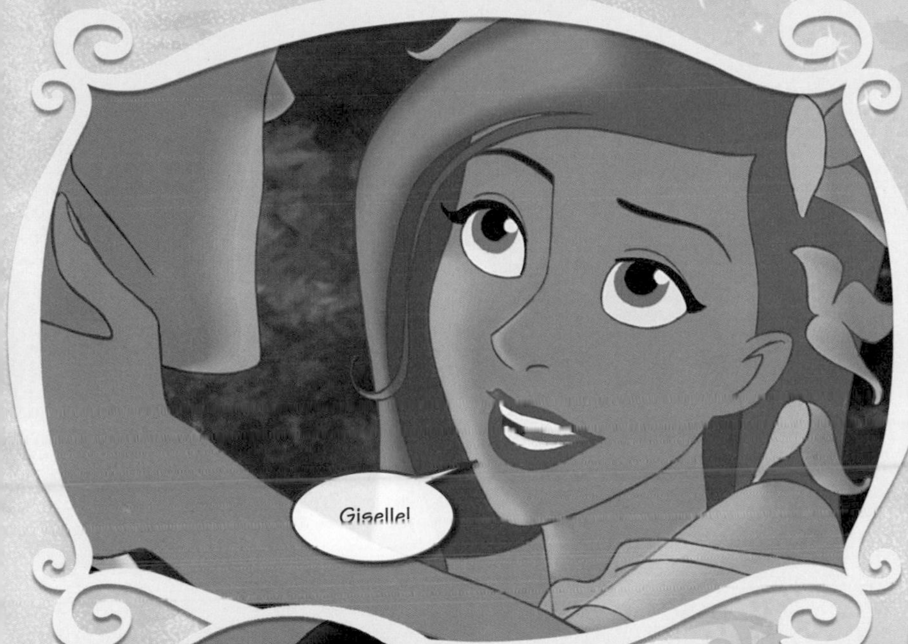
Giselle!

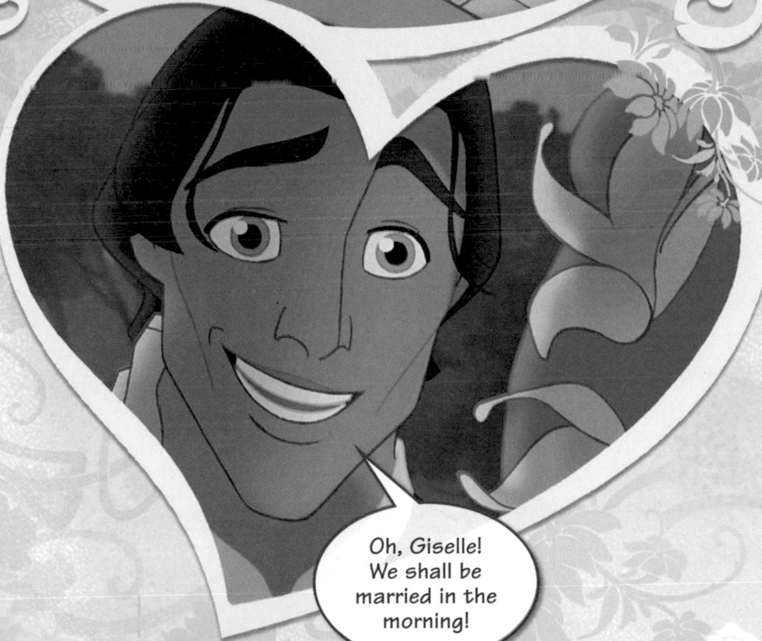
Oh, Giselle! We shall be married in the morning!

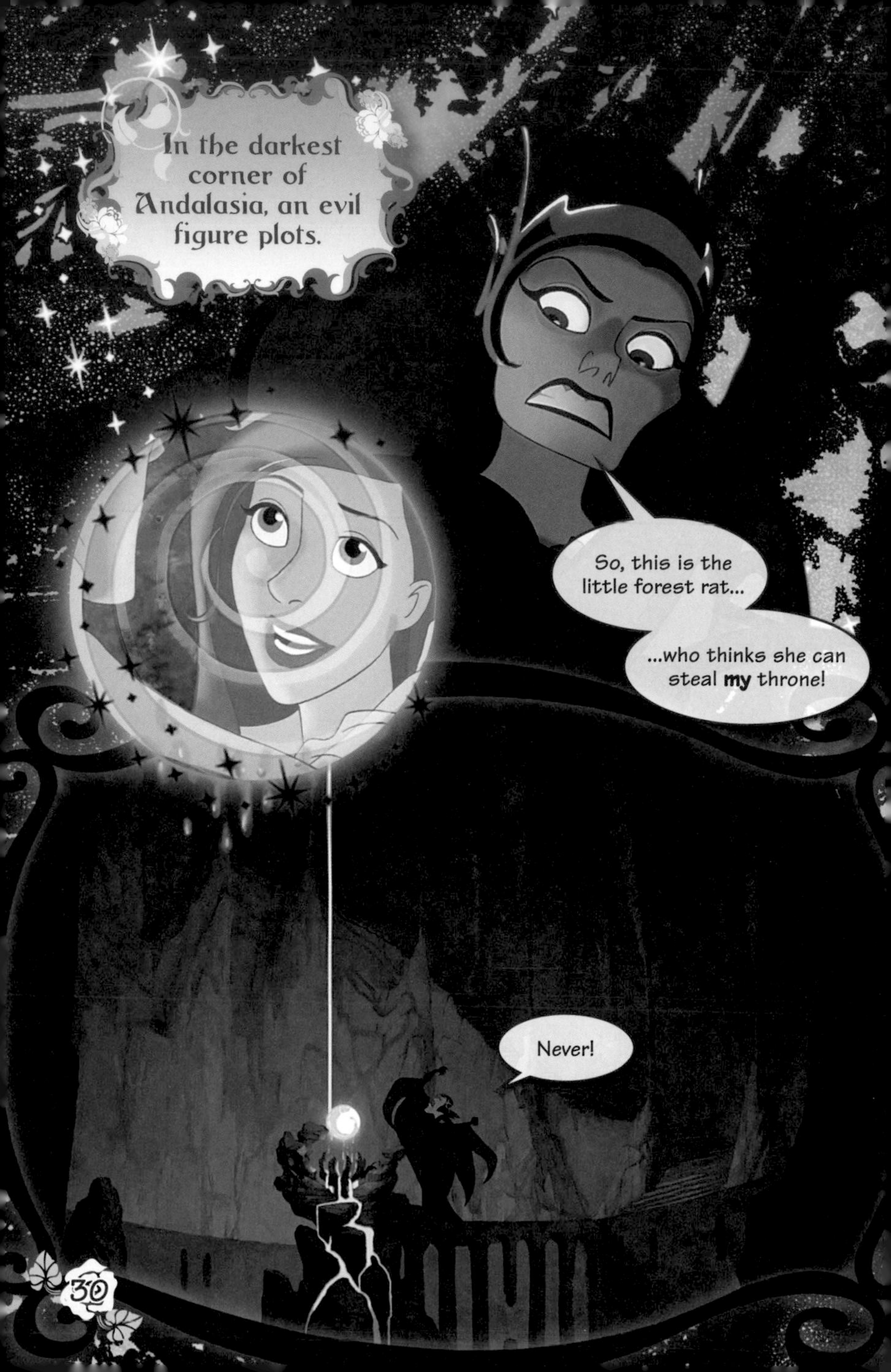

In the darkest corner of Andalasia, an evil figure plots.
So, this is the little forest rat...
...who thinks she can steal **my** throne!
Never!

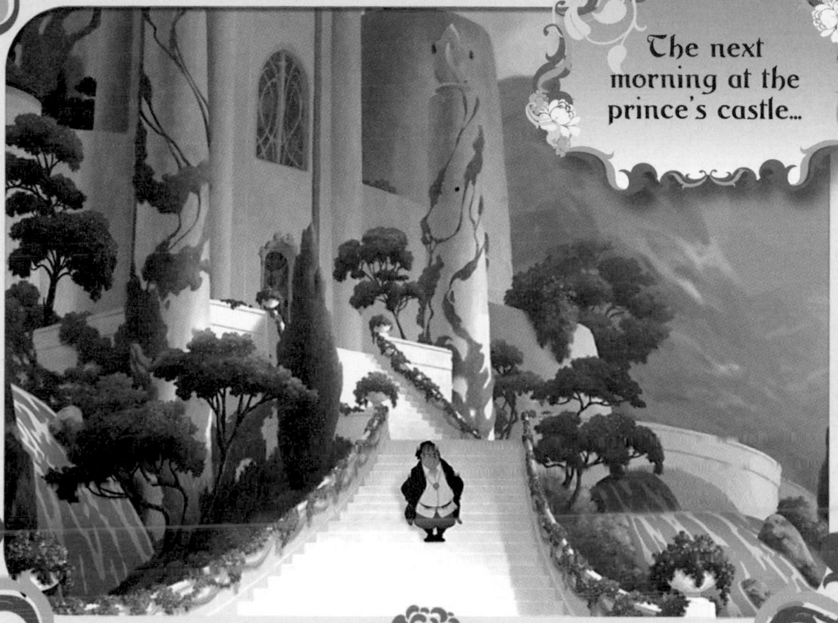
The next morning at the prince's castle...

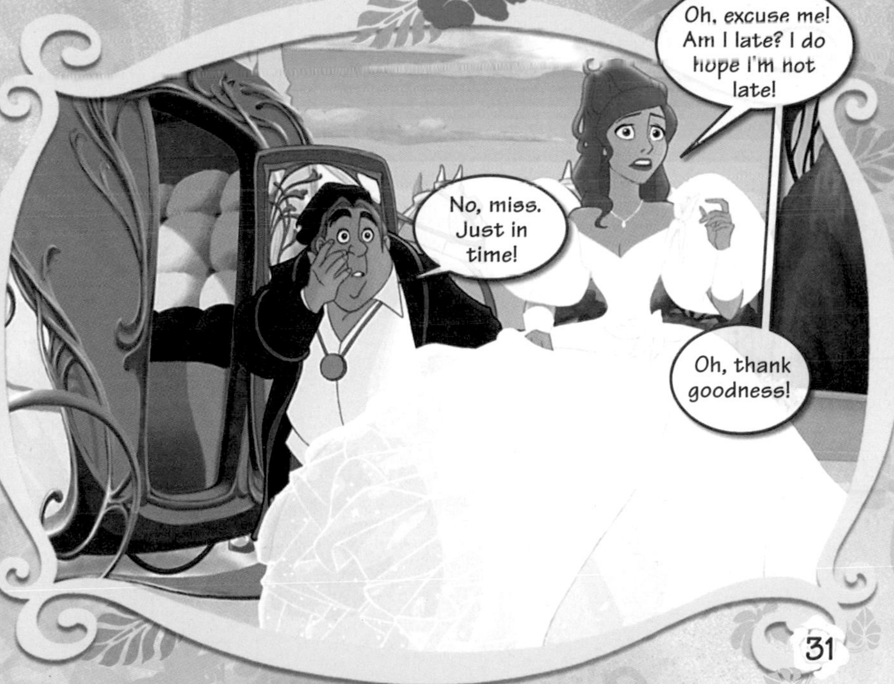
Oh, excuse me! Am I late? I do hope I'm not late!
No, miss. Just in time!
Oh, thank goodness!

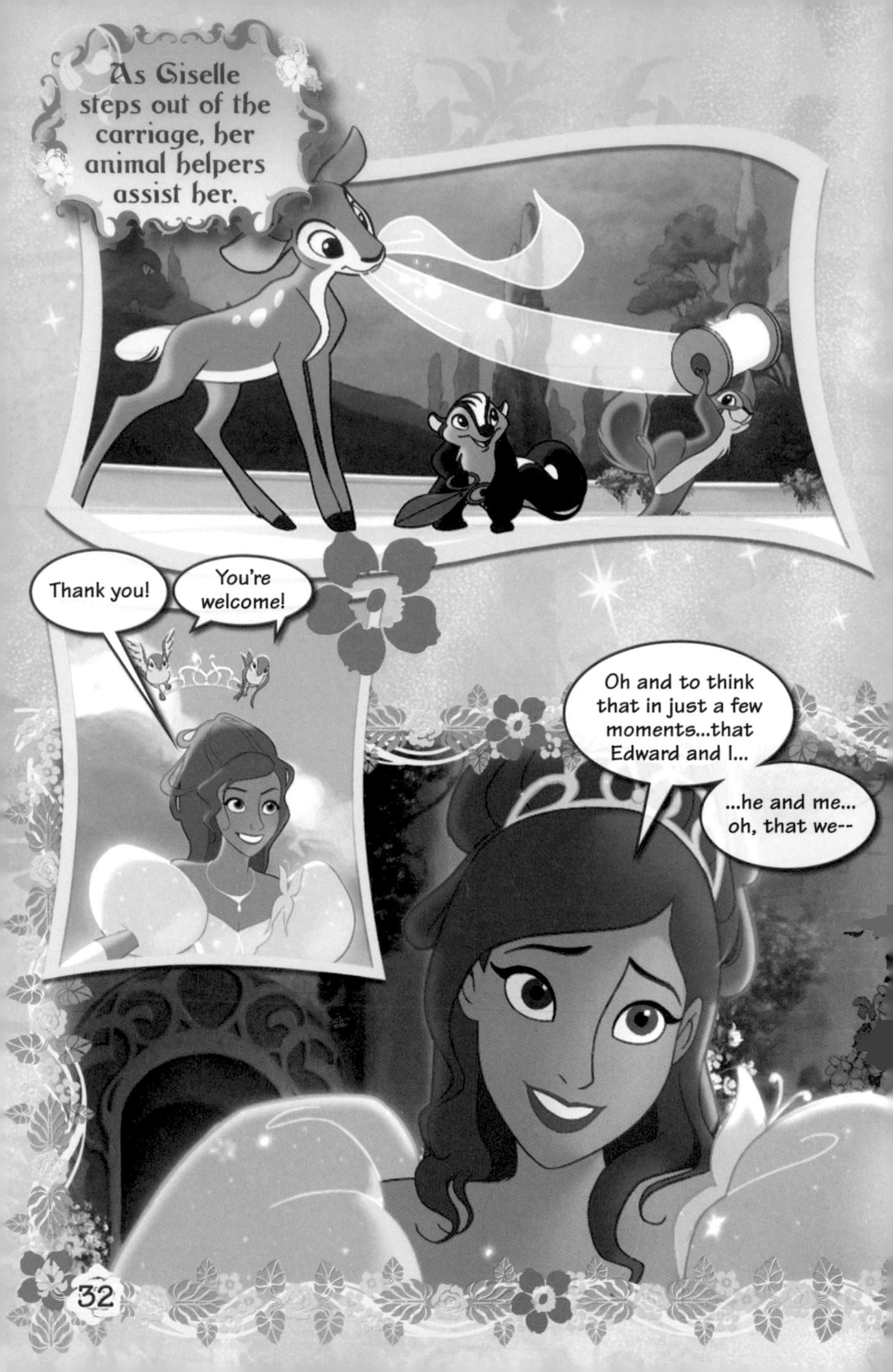
As Giselle steps out of the carriage, her animal helpers assist her.
Thank you!
You're welcome!
Oh and to think that in just a few moments...that Edward and I...
...he and me... oh, that we--

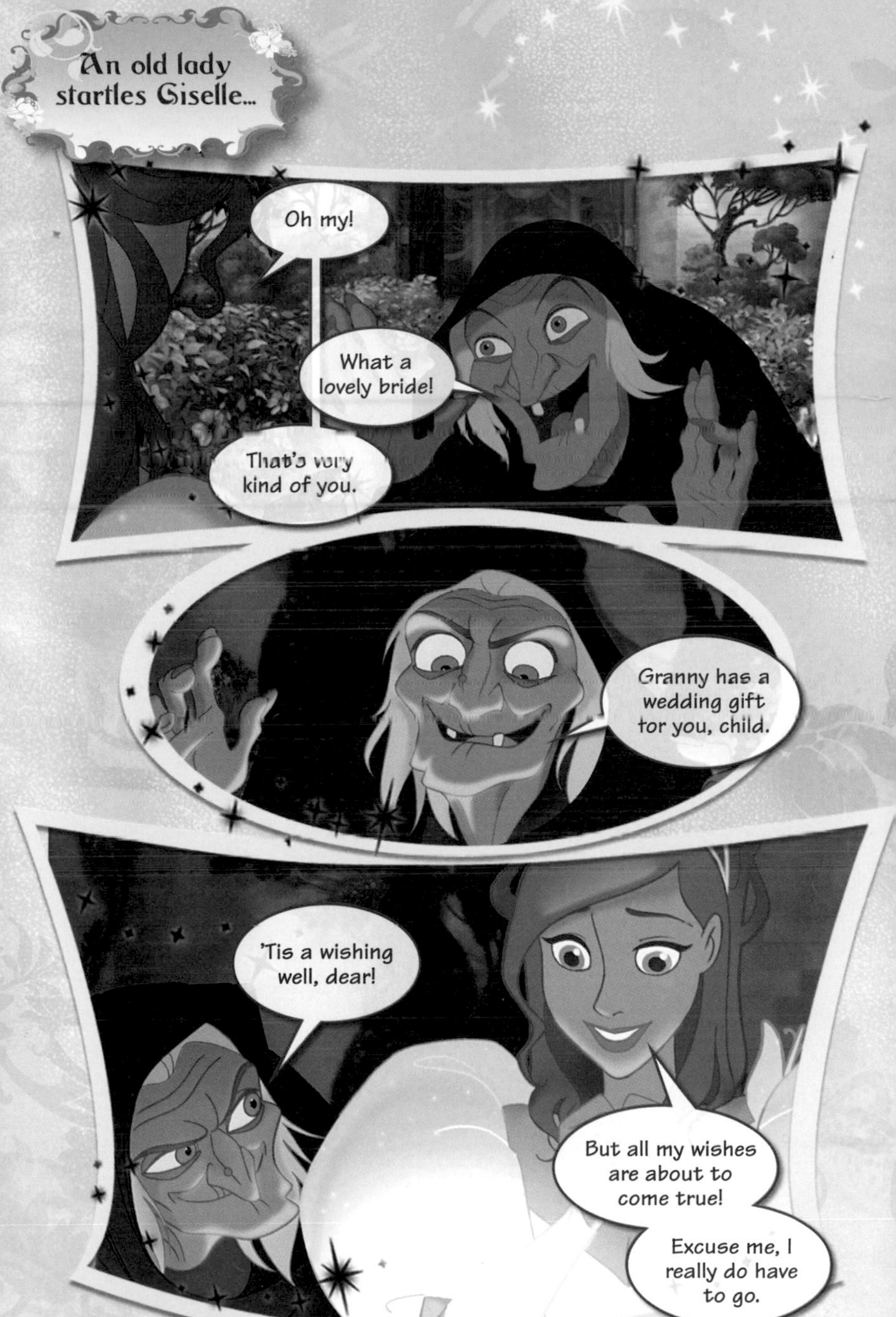
An old lady startles Giselle...
Oh my!
What a lovely bride!
That's very kind of you.
Granny has a wedding gift for you, child.
'Tis a wishing well, dear!
But all my wishes are about to come true!
Excuse me, I really do have to go.

But a wish on your wedding day! That's the most magical of all.

Just close your eyes, my darling, and make your wish. Are you wishing for something?
Yes, I am.
And just like that, the old woman pushes Giselle into the wishing well.

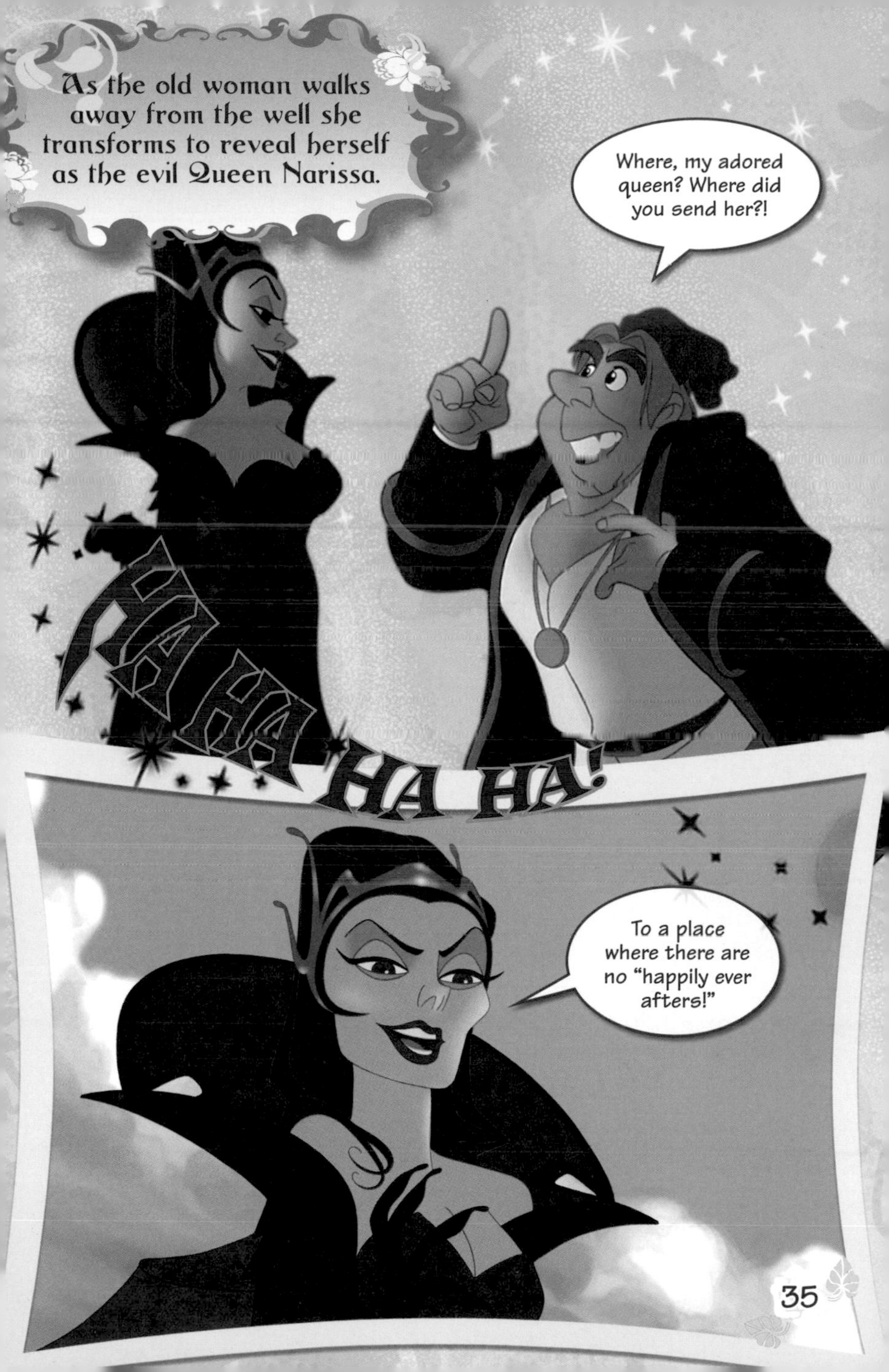
As the old woman walks away from the well she transforms to reveal herself as the evil Queen Narissa.
Where, my adored queen? Where did you send her?!
HA HA HA HA HA!
To a place where there are no "happily ever afters!"

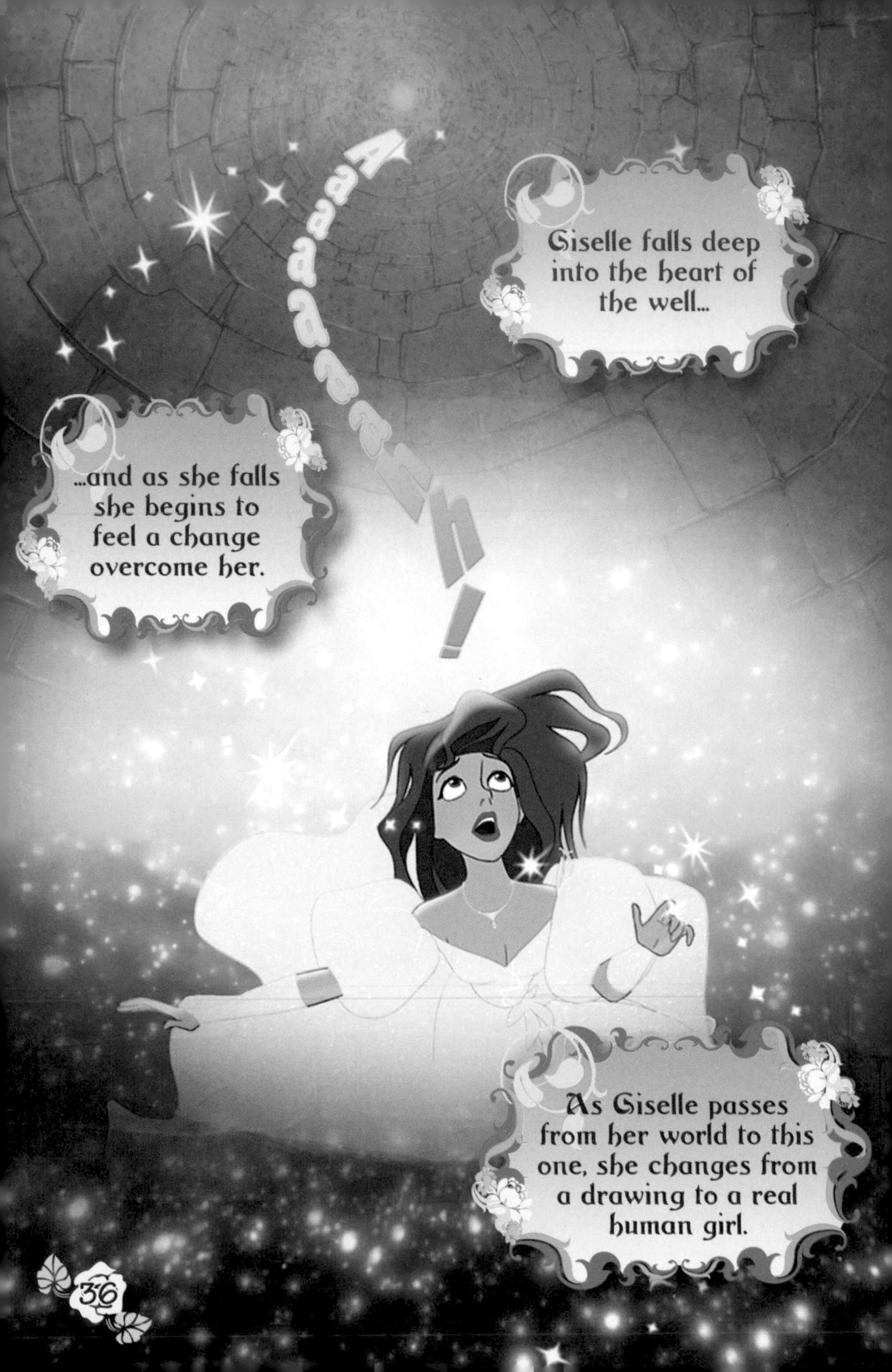
Giselle falls deep into the heart of the well...
Aaaaaaaaaah!
...and as she falls she begins to feel a change overcome her.
As Giselle passes from her world to this one, she changes from a drawing to a real human girl.

THUNK

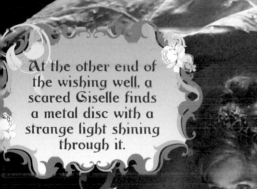

At the other end of the wishing well, a scared Giselle finds a metal disc with a strange light shining through it.

Oh my!

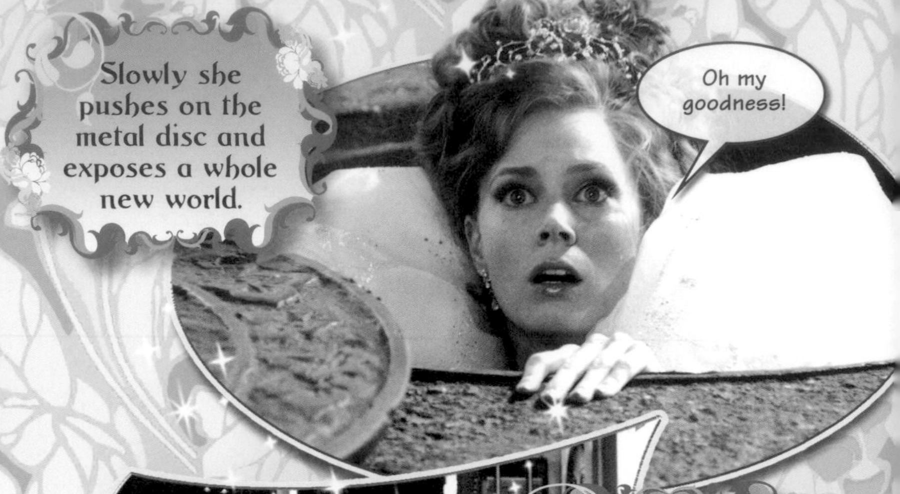
Slowly she pushes on the metal disc and exposes a whole new world.
Oh my goodness!
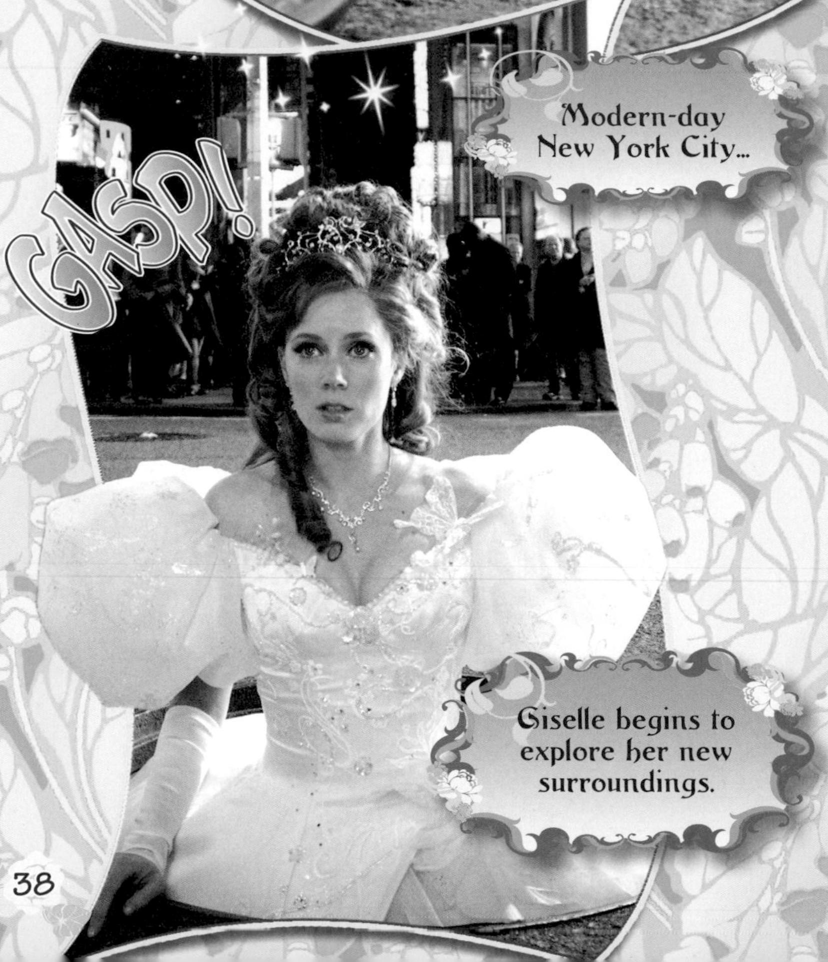
Modern-day New York City...
GASP!
Giselle begins to explore her new surroundings.

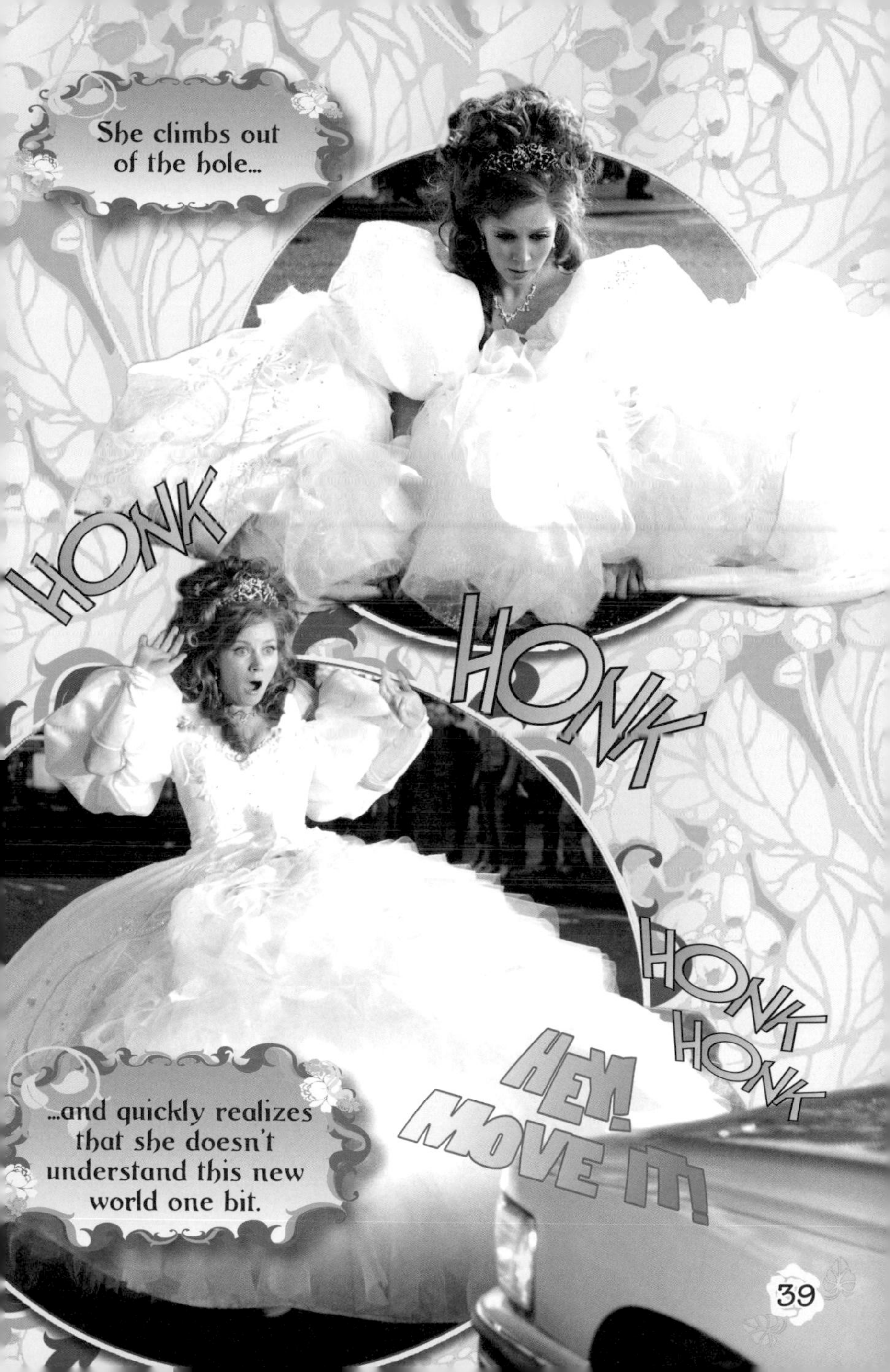
She climbs out of the hole...
HONK
HONK
HONK
HONK
HEY! MOVE IT!
...and quickly realizes that she doesn't understand this new world one bit.

Scared and confused, Giselle reaches out for help!

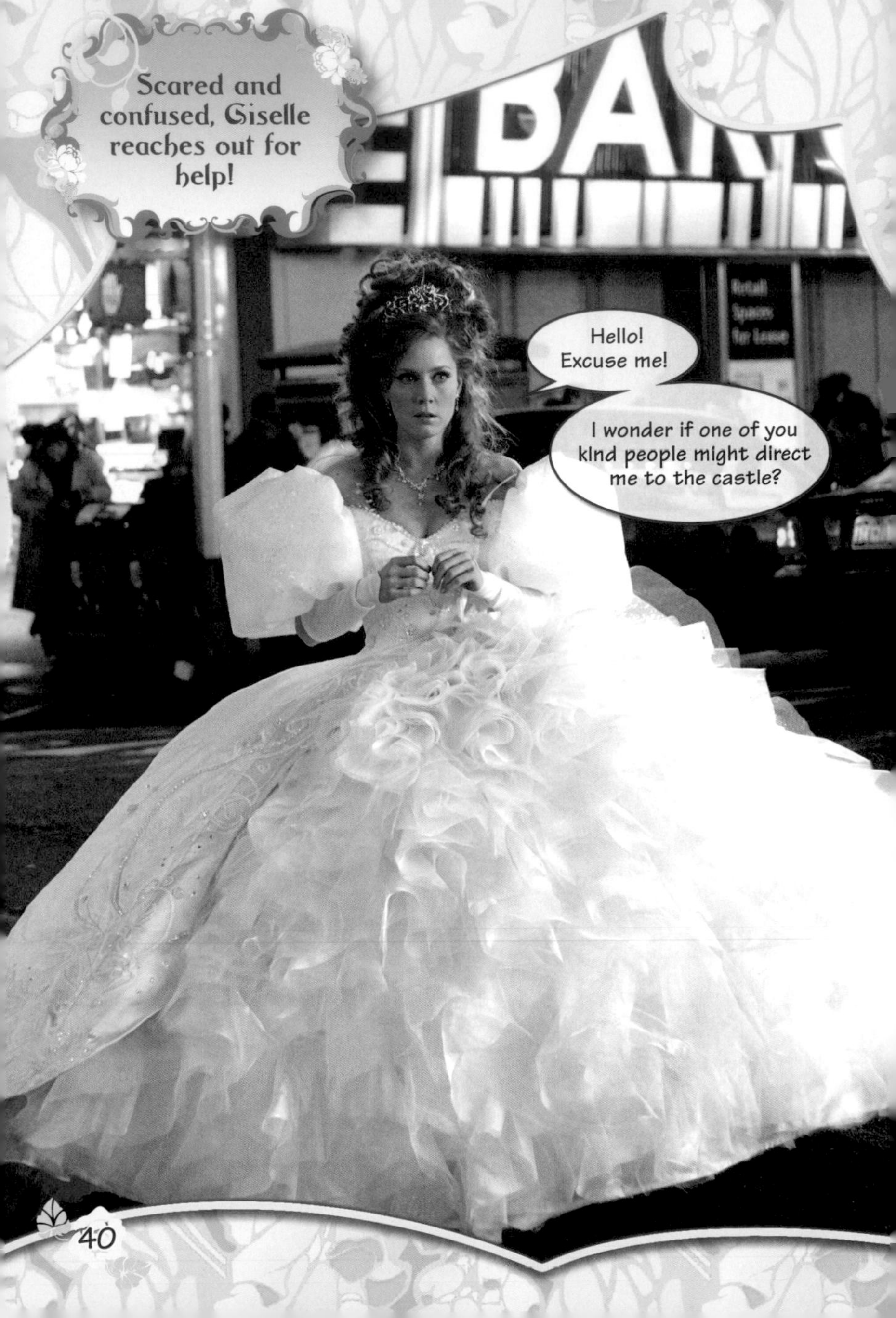
Hello! Excuse me!
I wonder if one of you kind people might direct me to the castle?

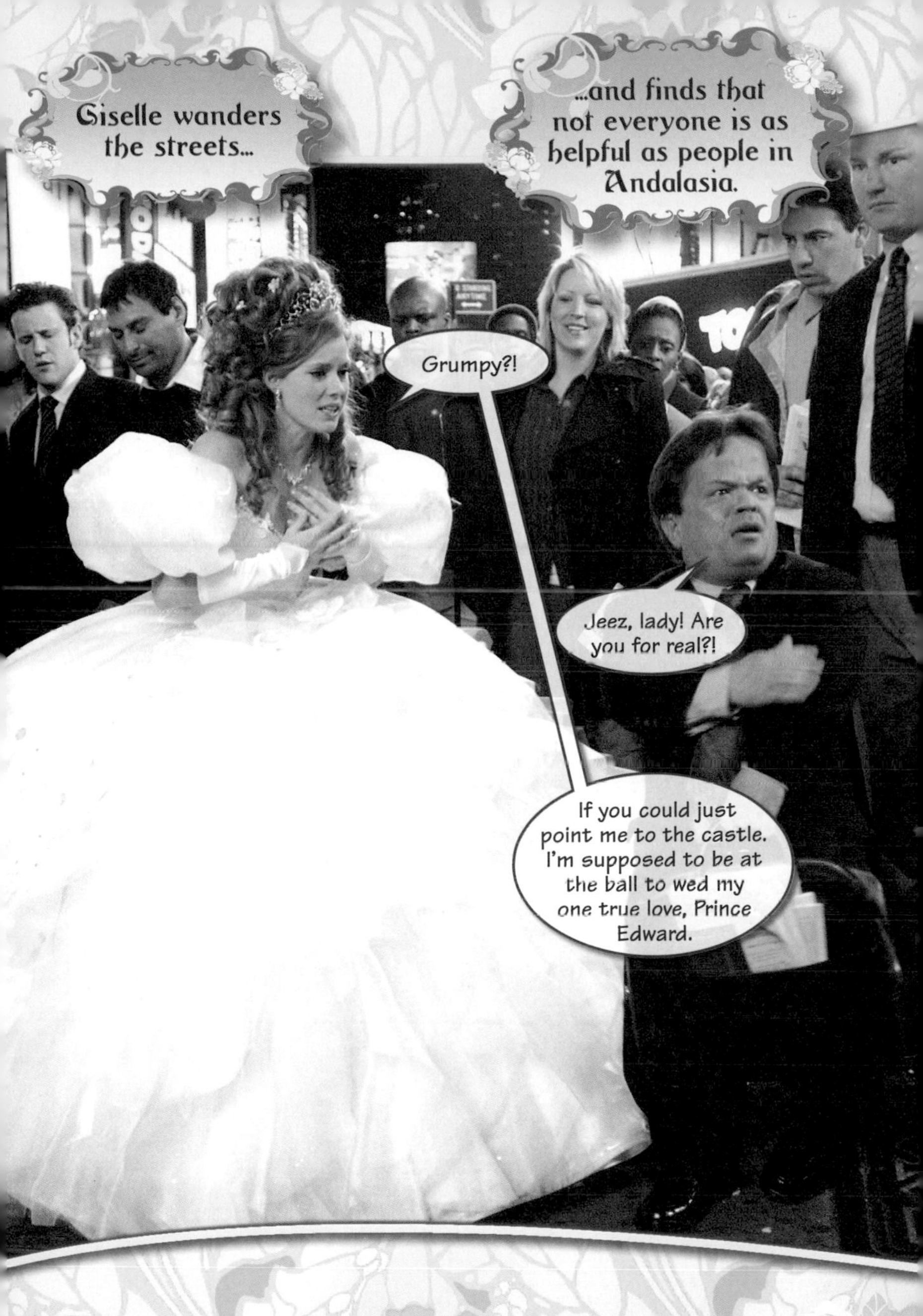
Giselle wanders the streets...
...and finds that not everyone is as helpful as people in Andalasia.
If you could just point me to the castle. I'm supposed to be at the ball to wed my one true love, Prince Edward.
Jeez, lady! Are you for real?!
Grumpy?!

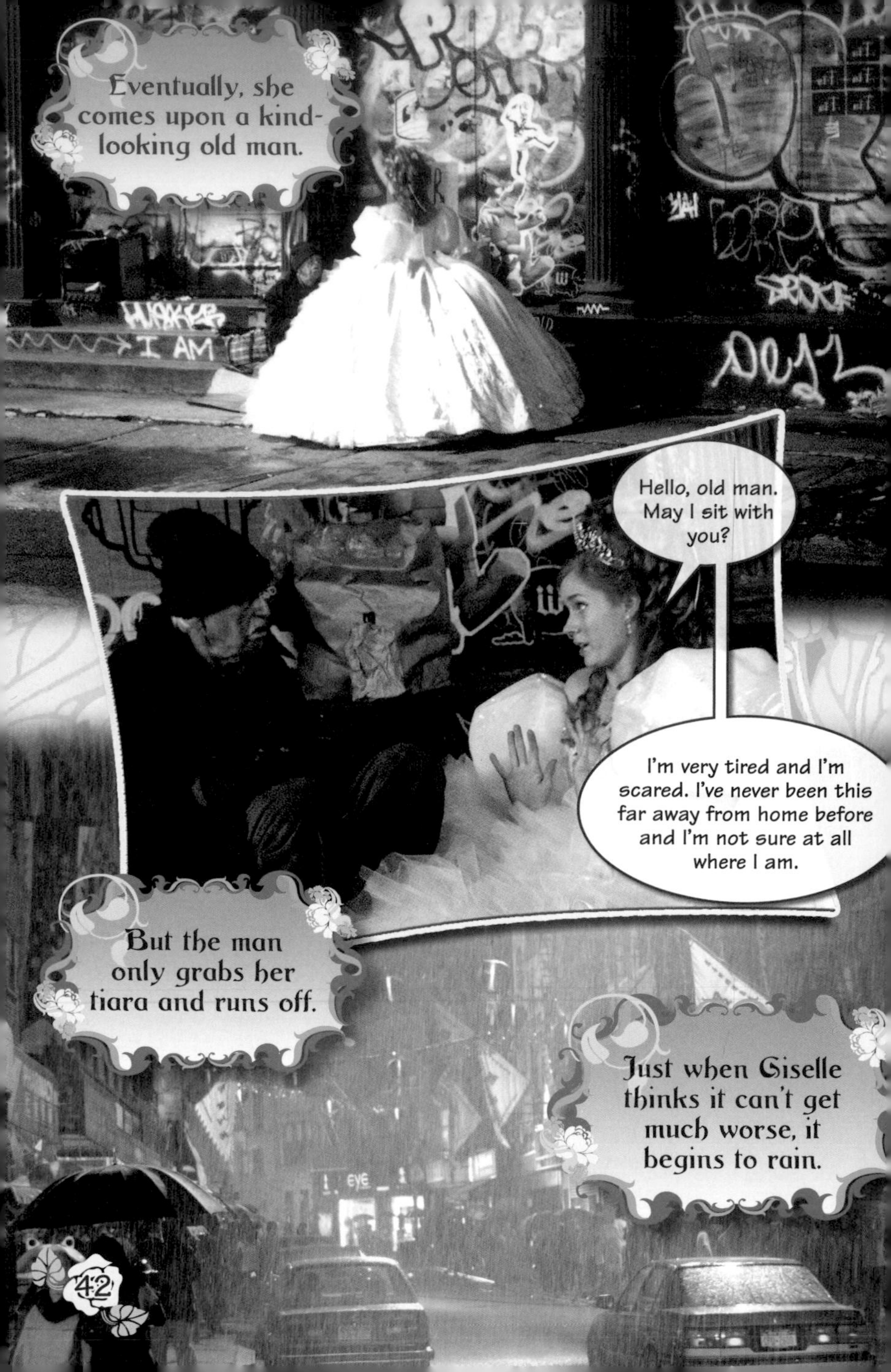
Eventually, she comes upon a kind-looking old man.
Hello, old man. May I sit with you?
I'm very tired and I'm scared. I've never been this far away from home before and I'm not sure at all where I am.
But the man only grabs her tiara and runs off.
Just when Giselle thinks it can't get much worse, it begins to rain.

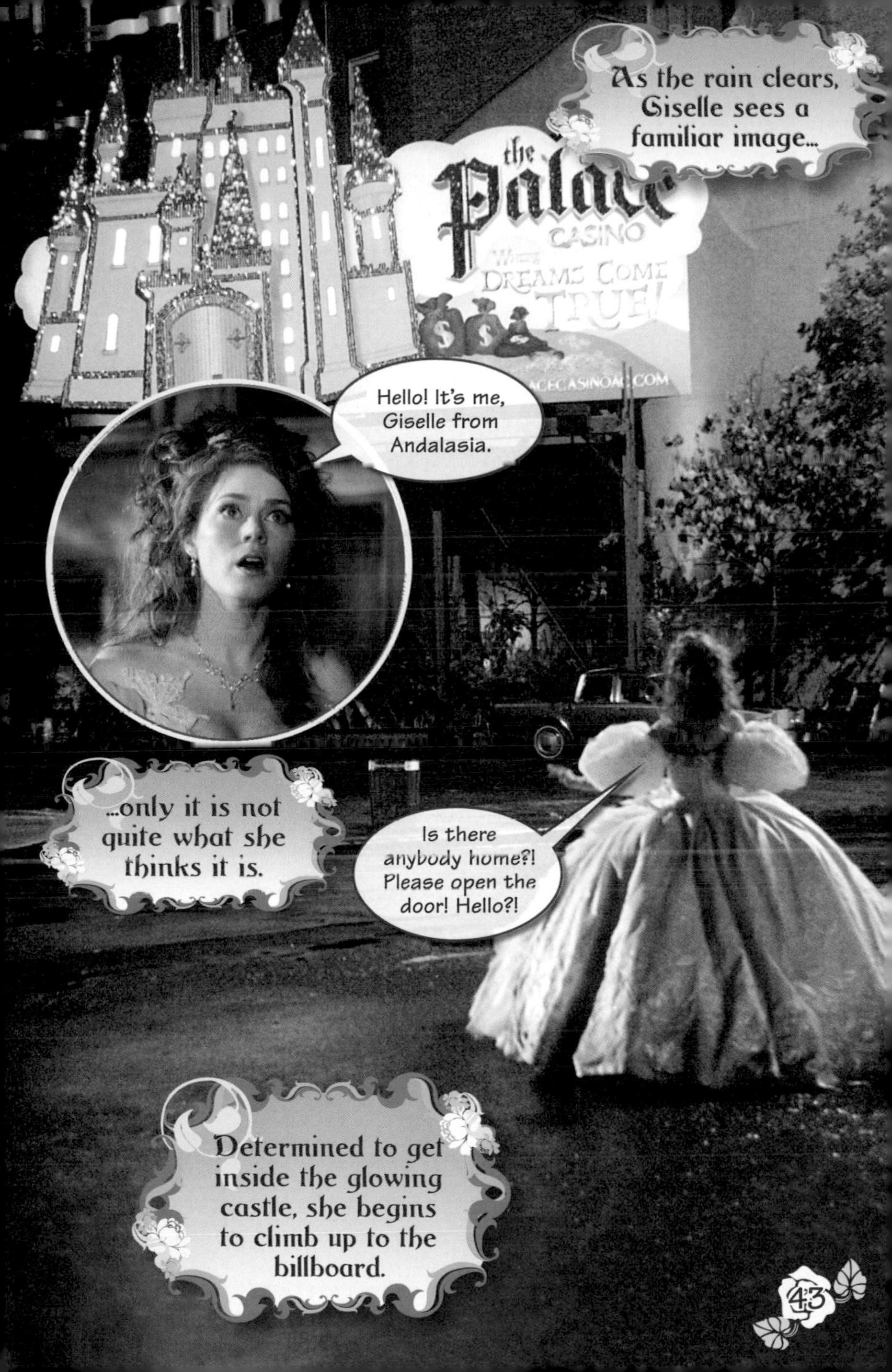
As the rain clears, Giselle sees a familiar image...
the Palace
CASINO
DREAMS COME TRUE!
Hello! It's me, Giselle from Andalasia.
...only it is not quite what she thinks it is.
Is there anybody home?! Please open the door! Hello?!
Determined to get inside the glowing castle, she begins to climb up to the billboard.

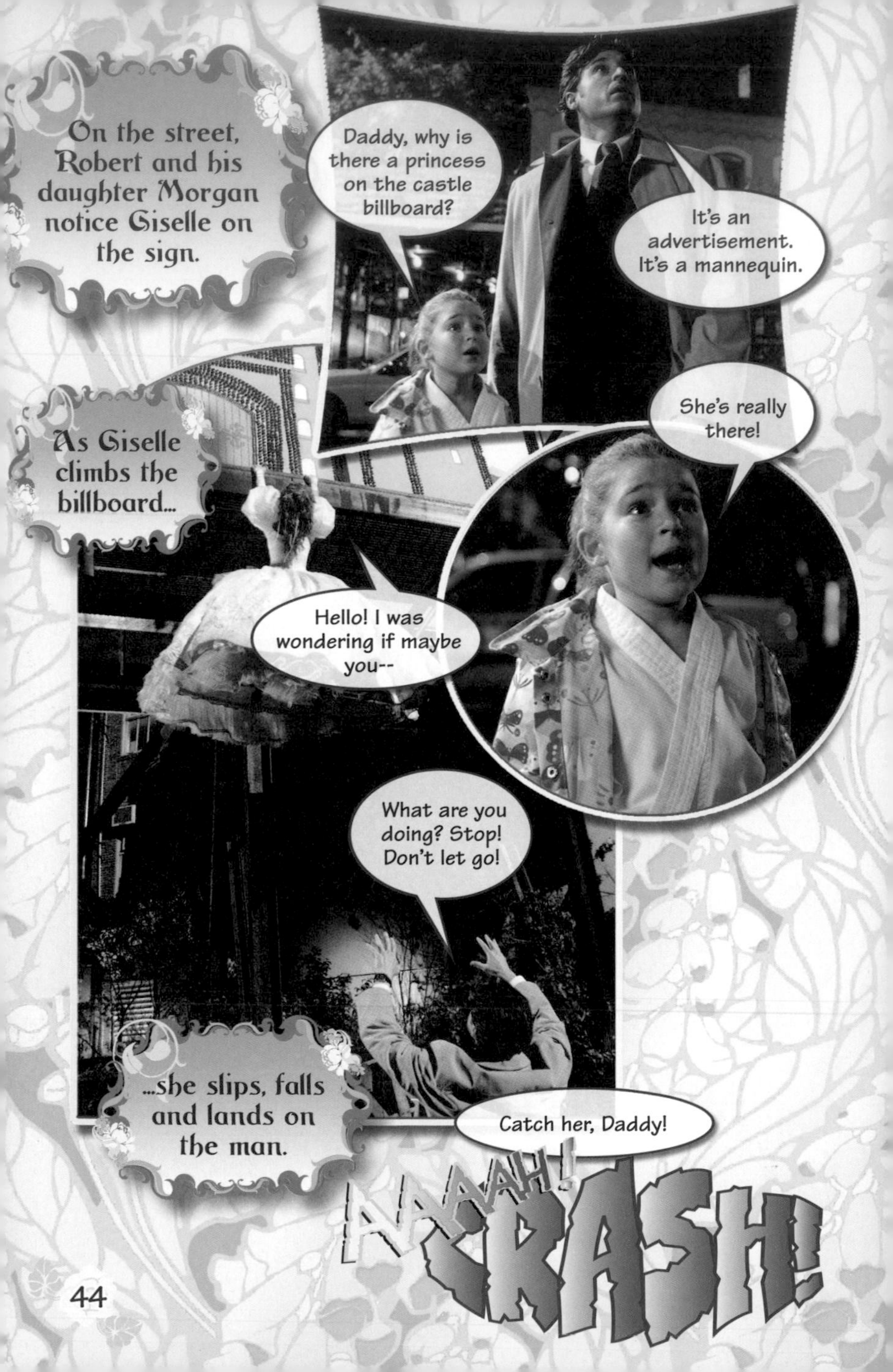
On the street, Robert and his daughter Morgan notice Giselle on the sign.
Daddy, why is there a princess on the castle billboard?
It's an advertisement. It's a mannequin.
She's really there!
As Giselle climbs the billboard...
Hello! I was wondering if maybe you--
What are you doing? Stop! Don't let go!
...she slips, falls and lands on the man.
Catch her, Daddy!
AAAAH!
CRASH!

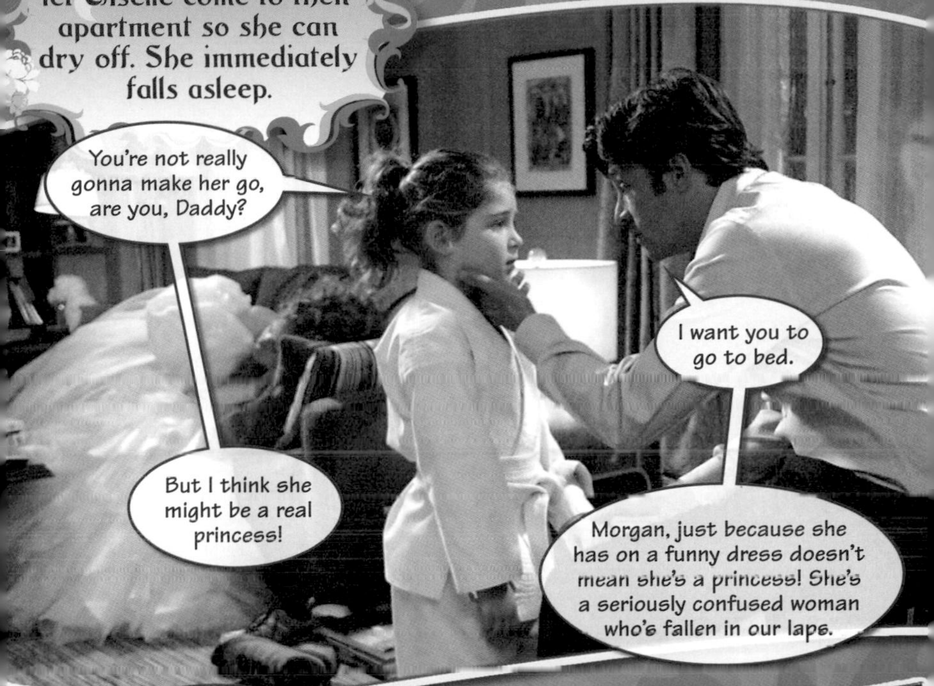
Robert and Morgan let Giselle come to their apartment so she can dry off. She immediately falls asleep.
You're not really gonna make her go, are you, Daddy?
I want you to go to bed.
But I think she might be a real princess!
Morgan, just because she has on a funny dress doesn't mean she's a princess! She's a seriously confused woman who's fallen in our laps.

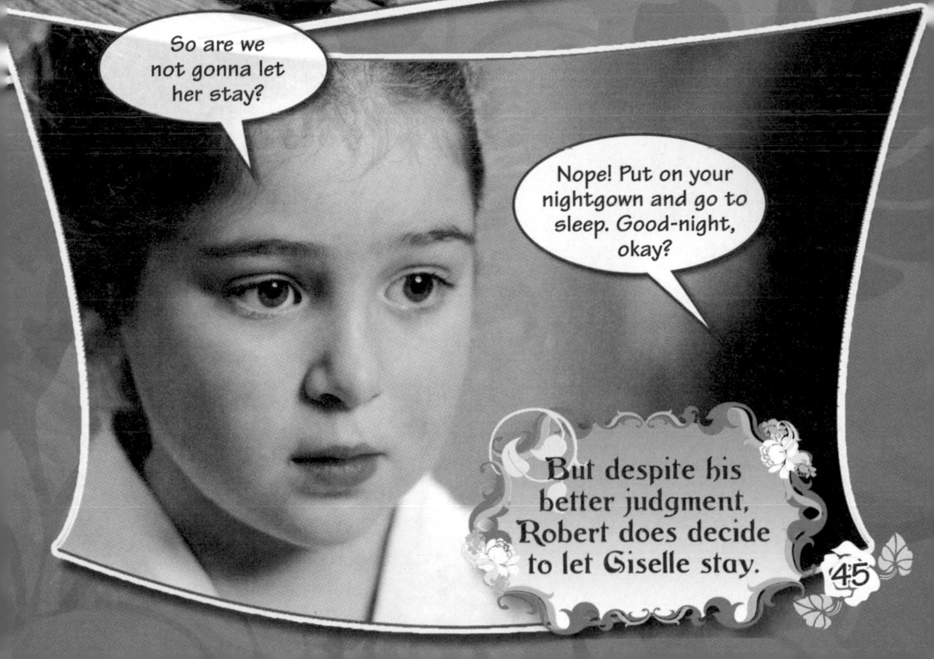
So are we not gonna let her stay?
Nope! Put on your nightgown and go to sleep. Good-night, okay?
But despite his better judgment, Robert does decide to let Giselle stay.

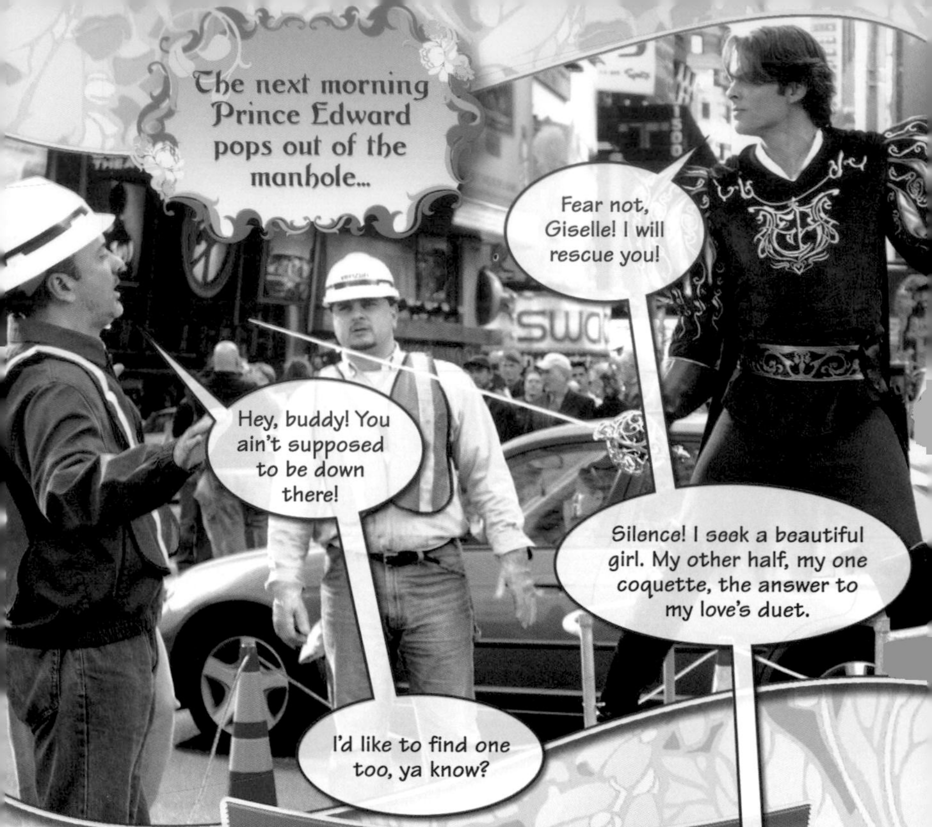
The next morning Prince Edward pops out of the manhole...
Fear not, Giselle! I will rescue you!
Hey, buddy! You ain't supposed to be down there!
Silence! I seek a beautiful girl. My other half, my one coquette, the answer to my love's duet.
I'd like to find one too, ya know?

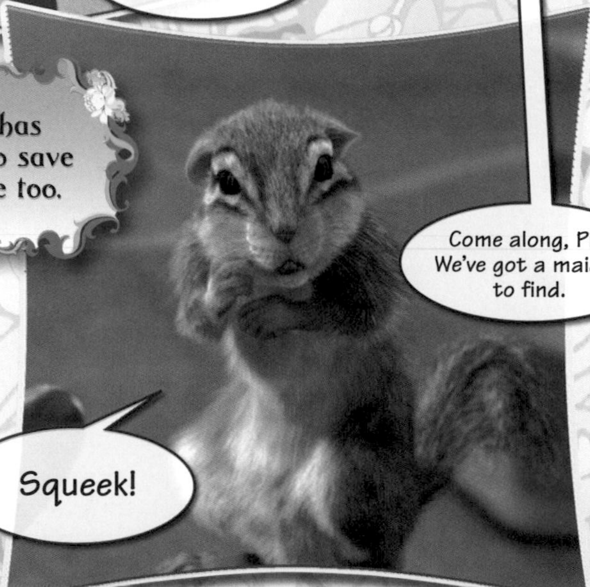
Pip has come to save Giselle too.
Come along, Pip. We've got a maiden to find.
Squeek!

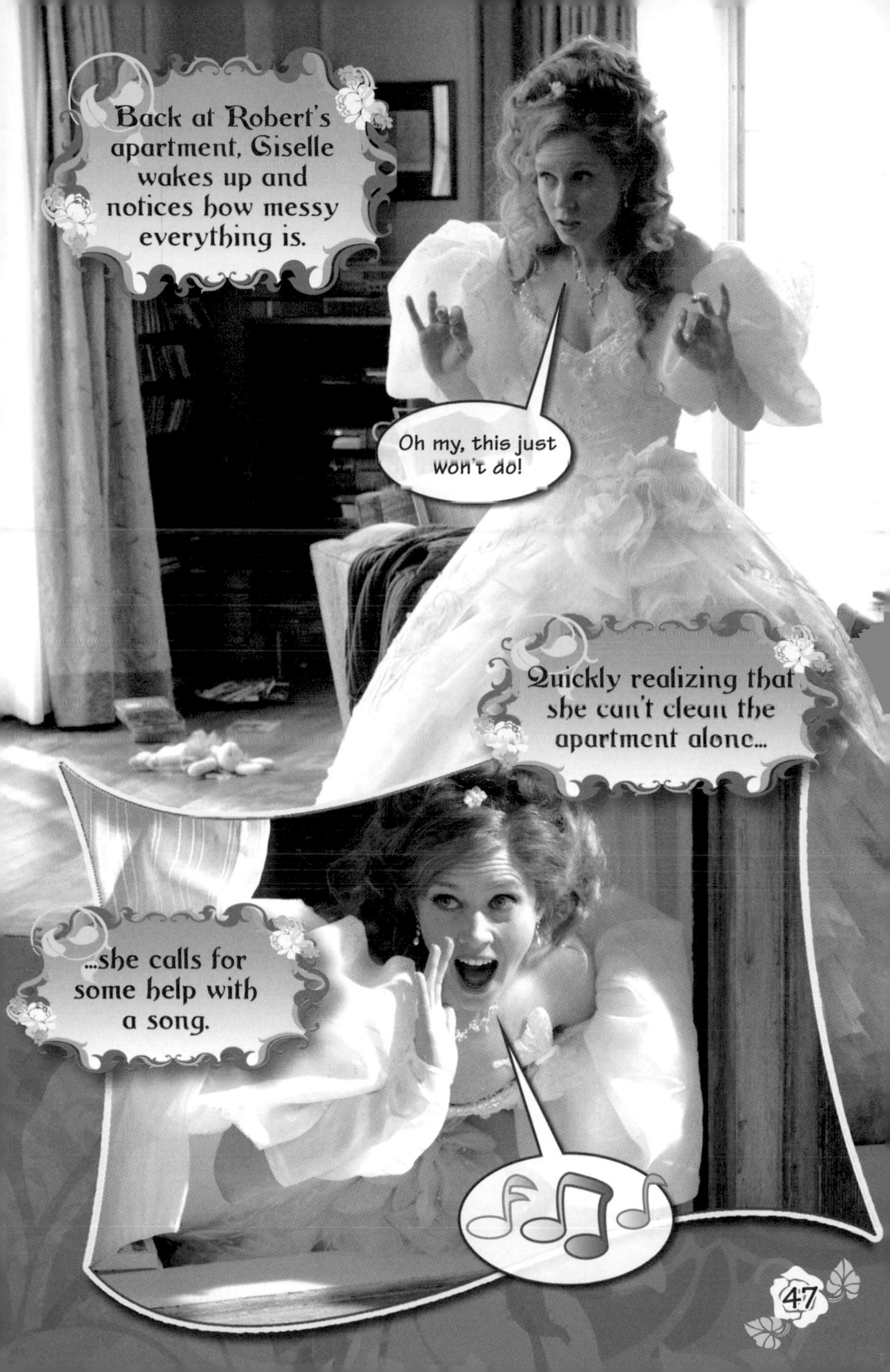
Back at Robert's apartment, Giselle wakes up and notices how messy everything is.
Oh my, this just won't do!
Quickly realizing that she can't clean the apartment alone...
...she calls for some help with a song.

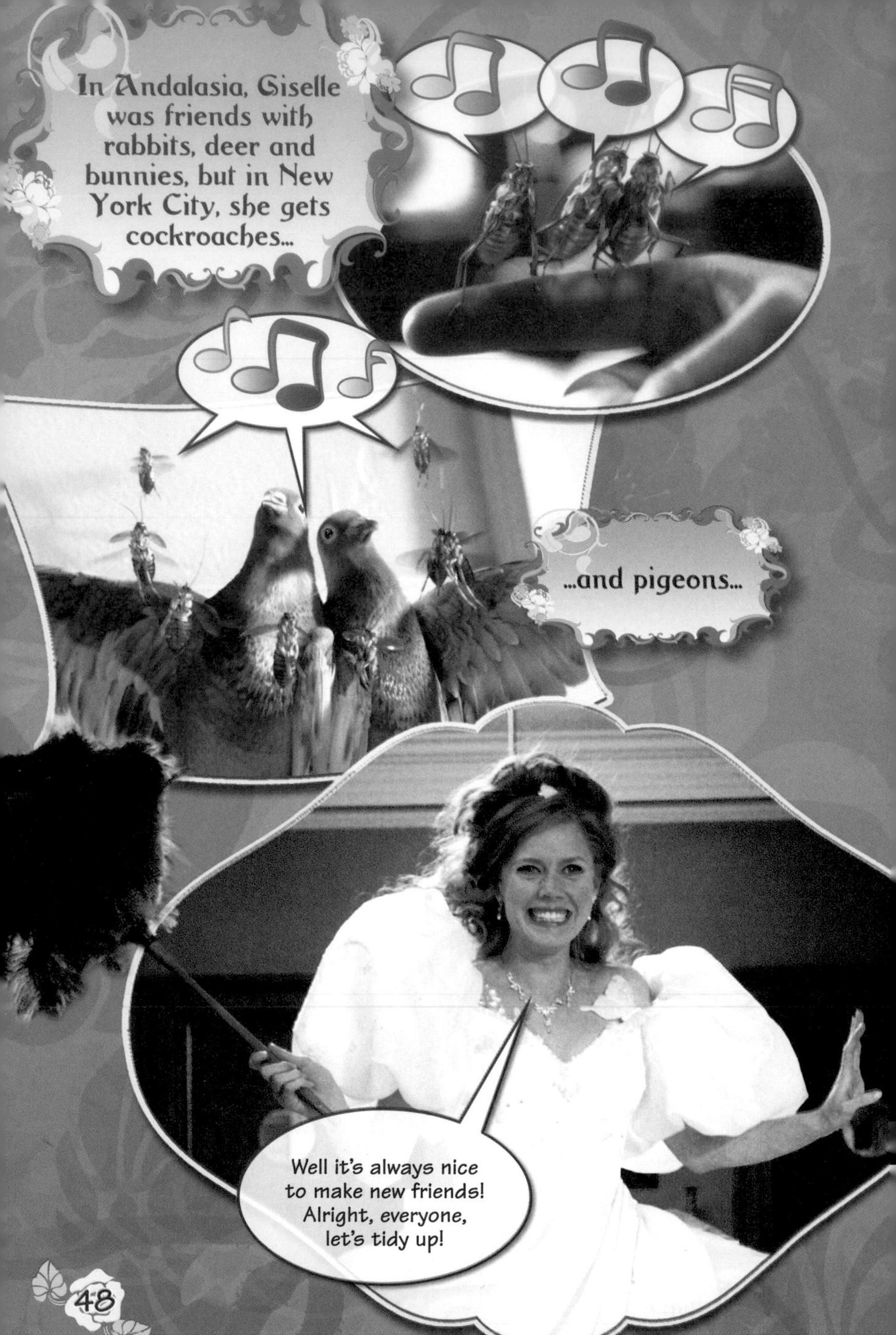
In Andalasia, Giselle was friends with rabbits, deer and bunnies, but in New York City, she gets cockroaches...
...and pigeons...
Well it's always nice to make new friends! Alright, everyone, let's tidy up!

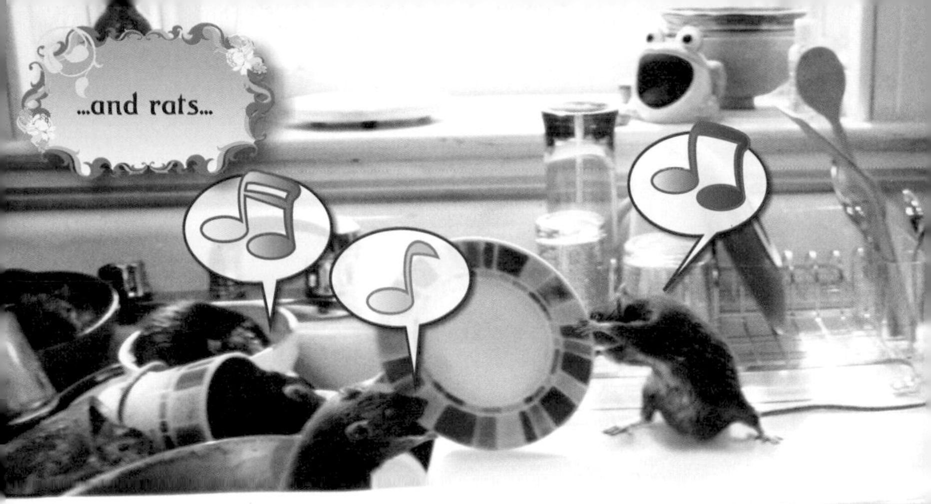
...and rats...

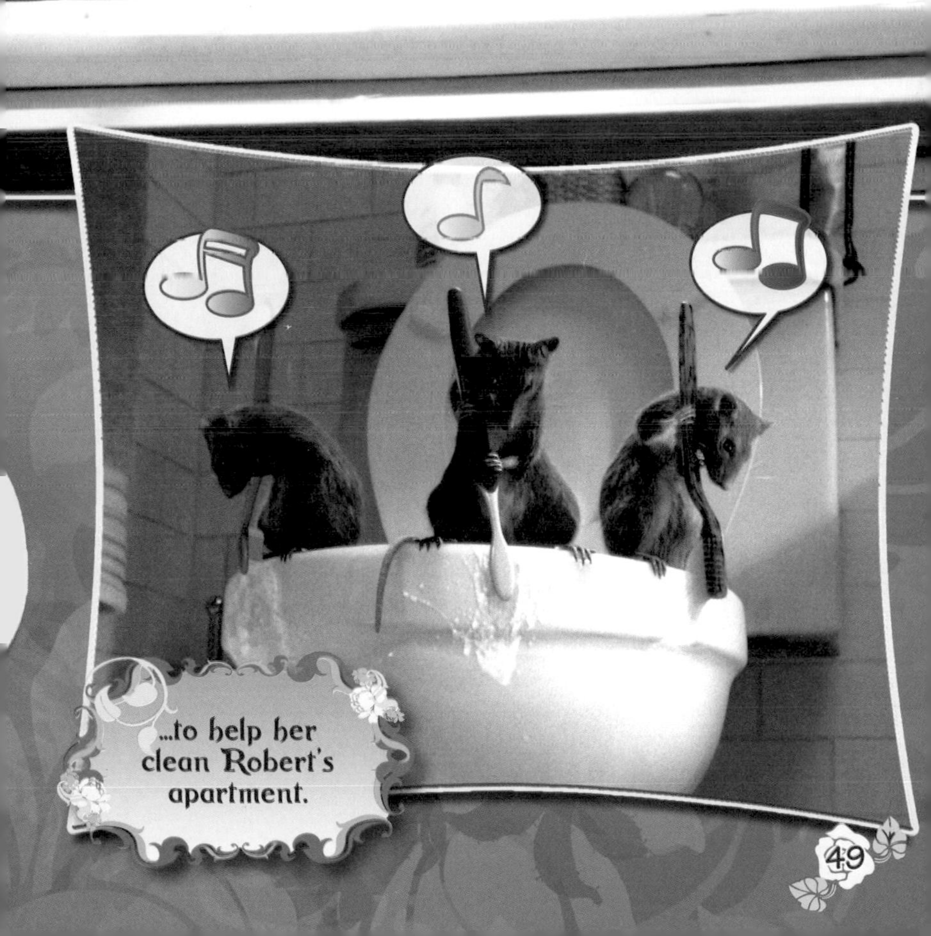
...to help her
clean Robert's
apartment.

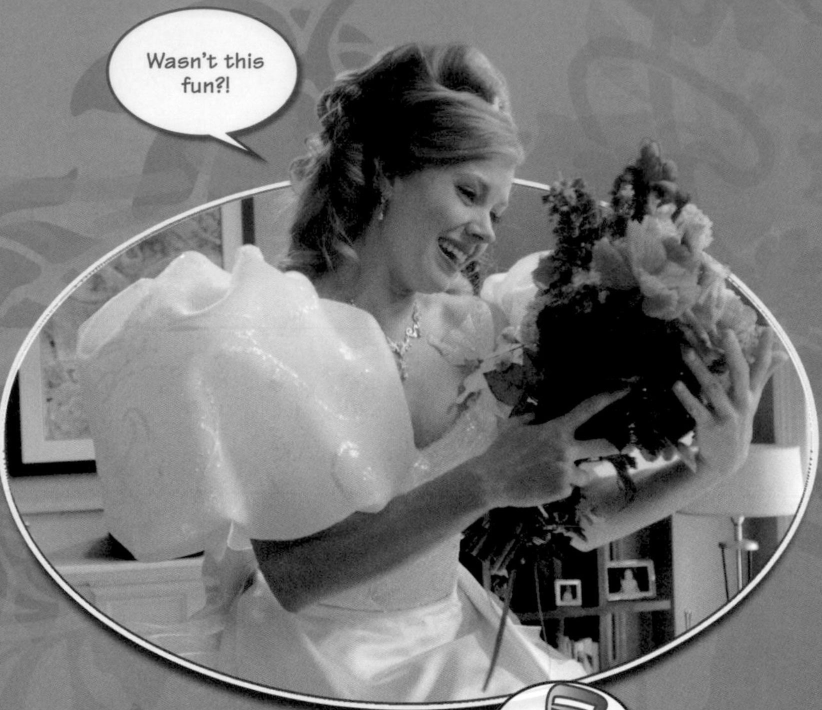
Wasn't this fun?!

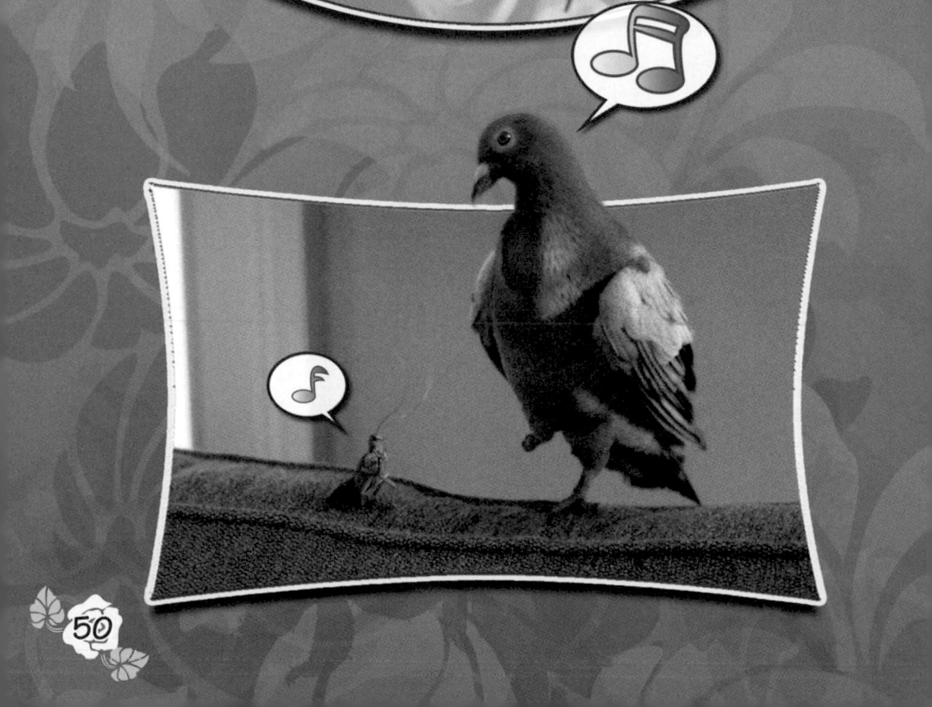

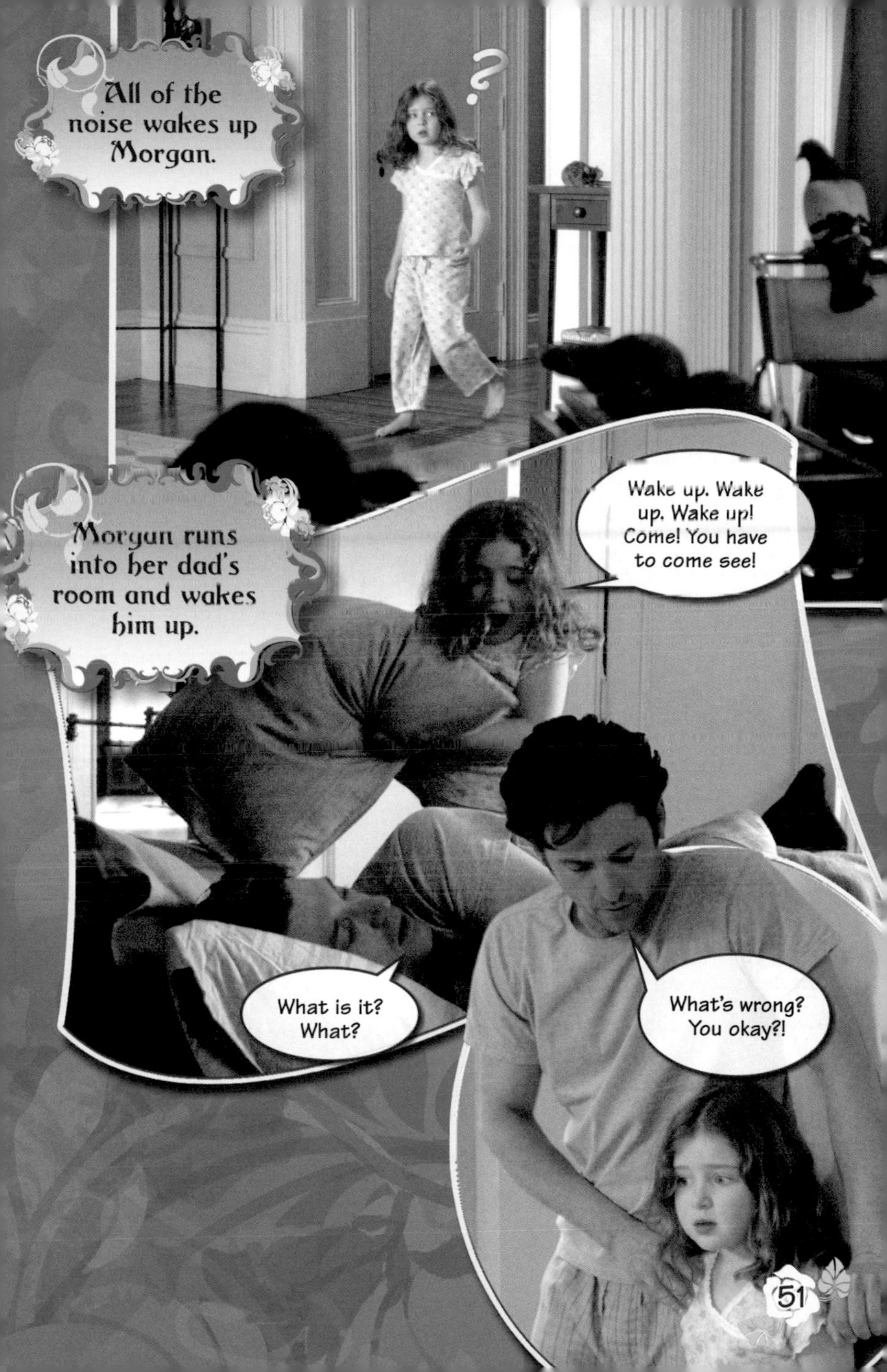
All of the noise wakes up Morgan.
Morgan runs into her dad's room and wakes him up.
Wake up. Wake up. Wake up! Come! You have to come see!
What is it? What?
What's wrong? You okay?!

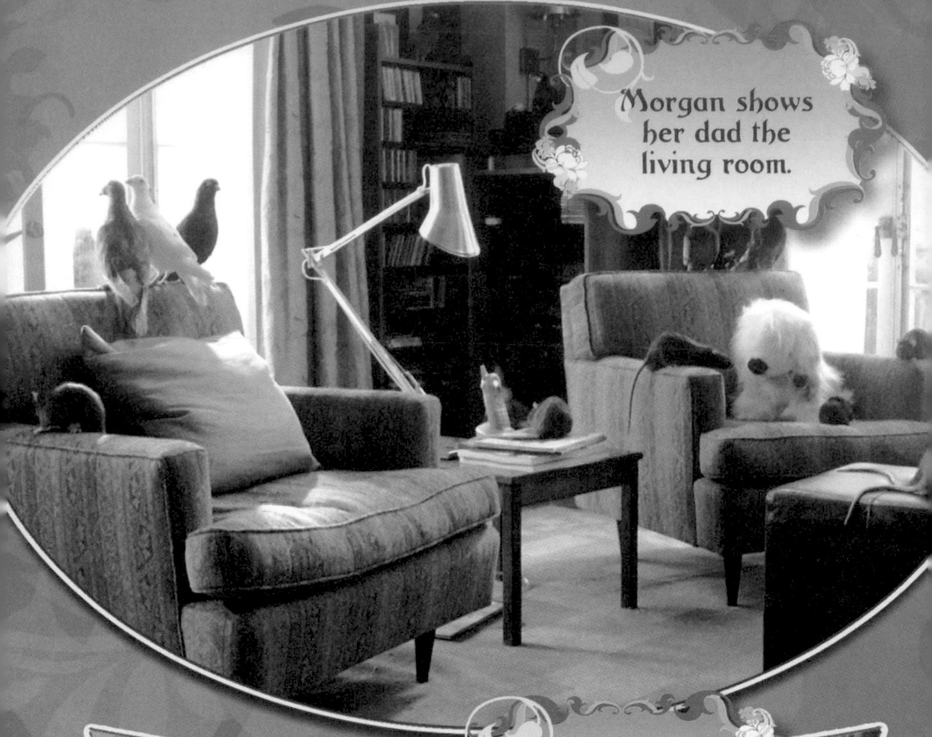
Morgan shows her dad the living room.

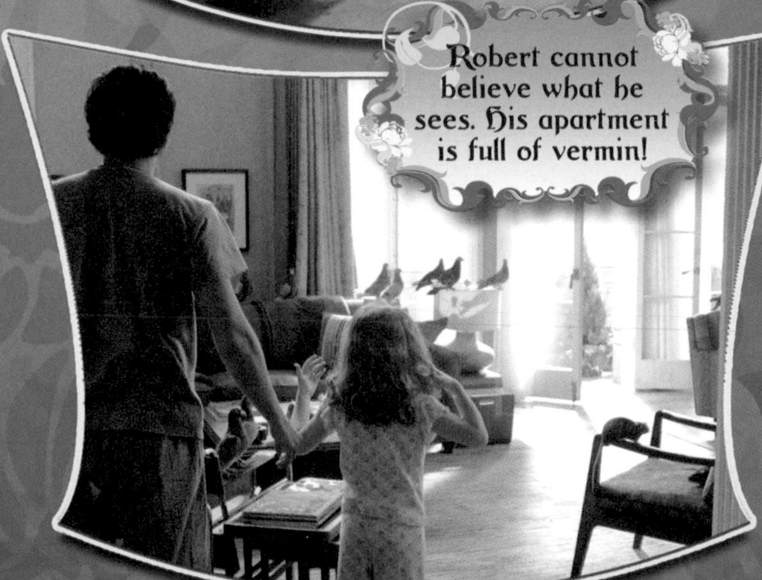
Robert cannot believe what he sees. His apartment is full of vermin!

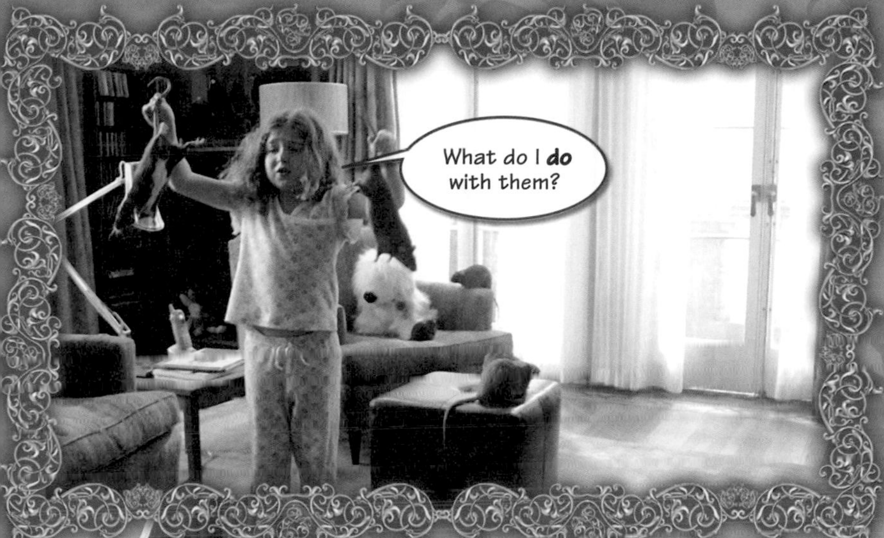
What do I **do** with them?

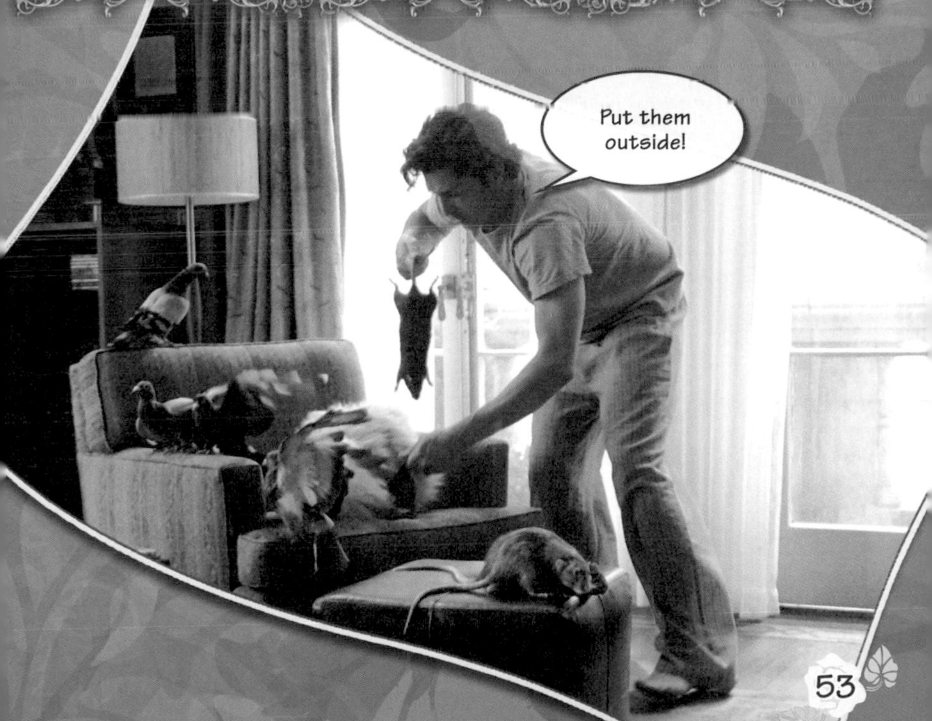
Put them outside!

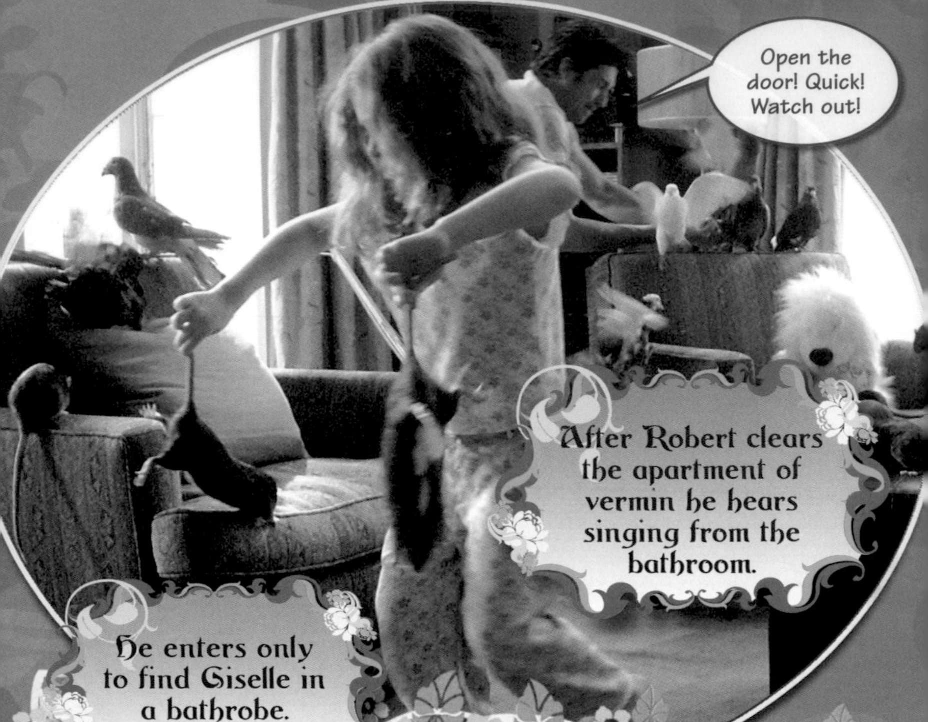
Open the door! Quick! Watch out!
After Robert clears the apartment of vermin he hears singing from the bathroom.

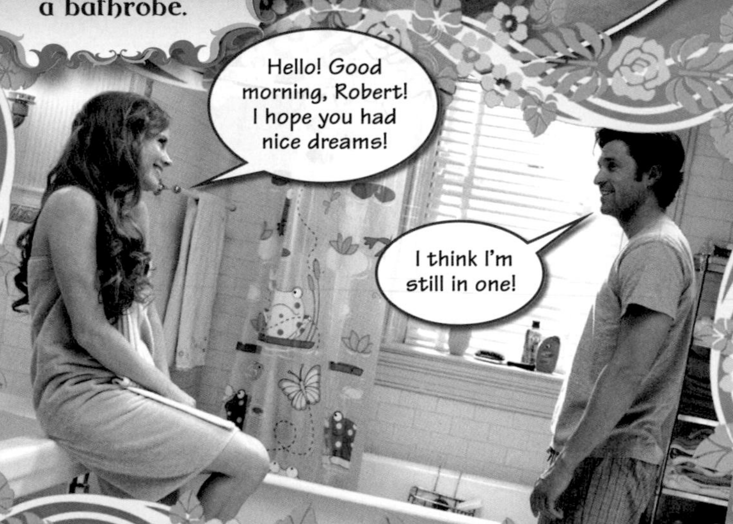
He enters only to find Giselle in a bathrobe.
Hello! Good morning, Robert! I hope you had nice dreams!
I think I'm still in one!

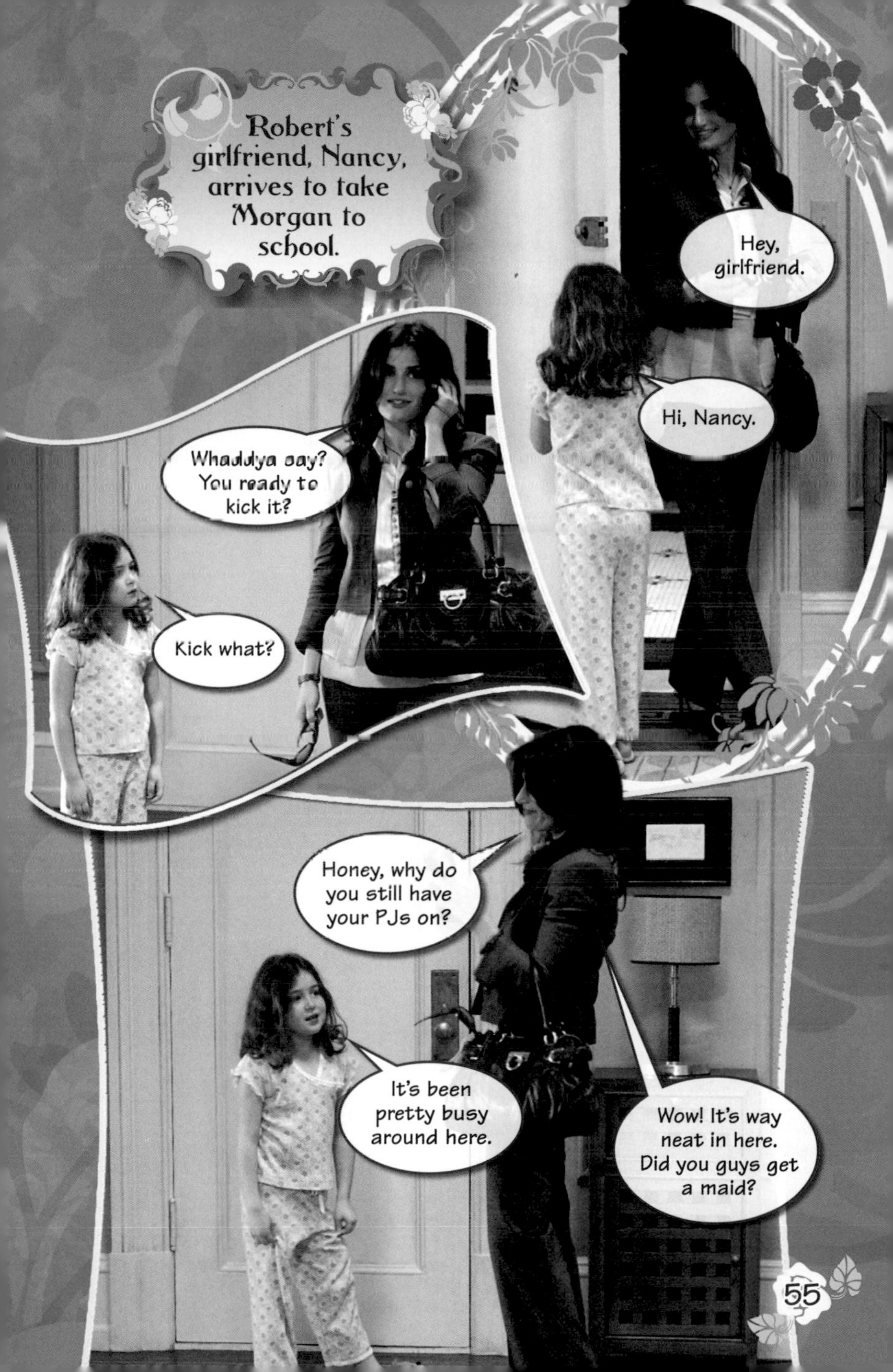
Robert's girlfriend, Nancy, arrives to take Morgan to school.
Hey, girlfriend.
Hi, Nancy.
Whaddya say? You ready to kick it?
Kick what?
Honey, why do you still have your PJs on?
It's been pretty busy around here.
Wow! It's way neat in here. Did you guys get a maid?

Robert and Giselle emerge from the bathroom and find Nancy.

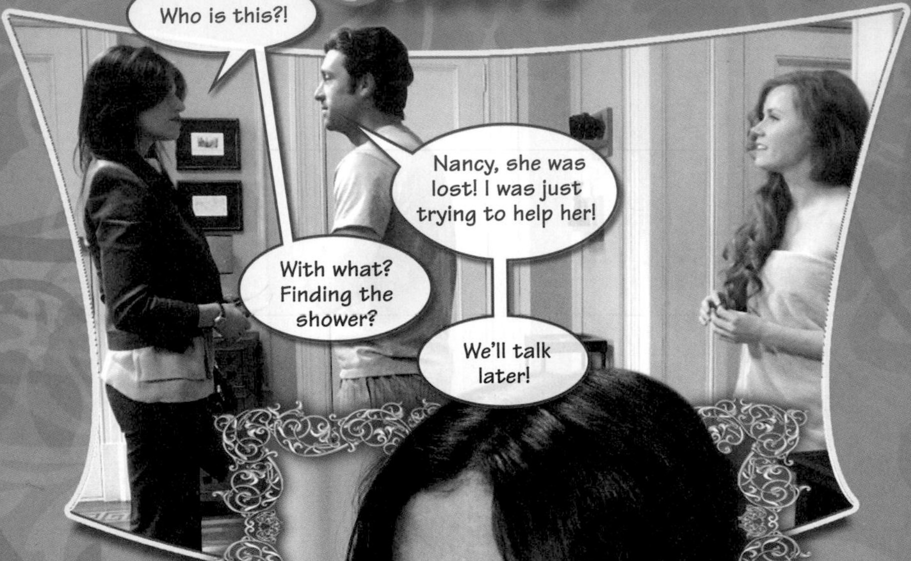
Who is this?!
Nancy, she was lost! I was just trying to help her!
With what? Finding the shower?
We'll talk later!

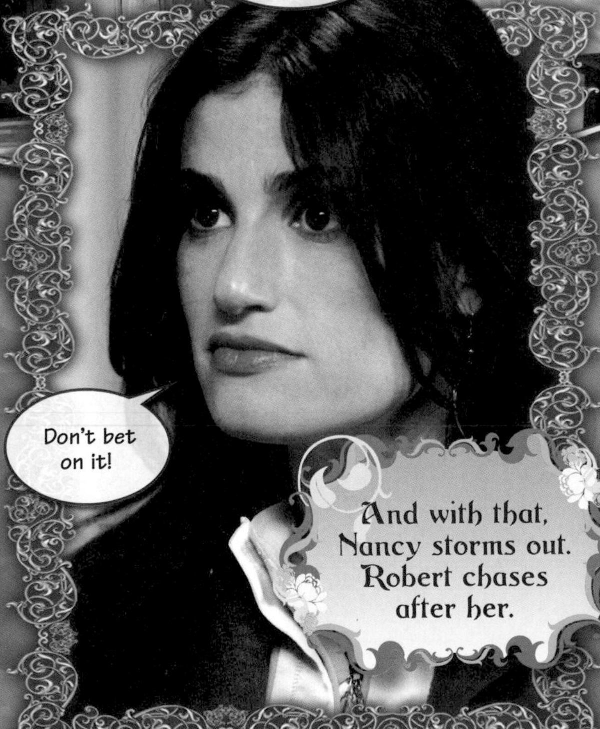
Don't bet on it!
And with that, Nancy storms out. Robert chases after her.

When Robert returns, he sees Giselle in a new dress.
Where did you get that dress?
I made it! You're unhappy?
You made a dress out of my curtains--?
School! We're late! We gotta run!
Robert changes and runs out the door to get Morgan to school with Giselle close behind.

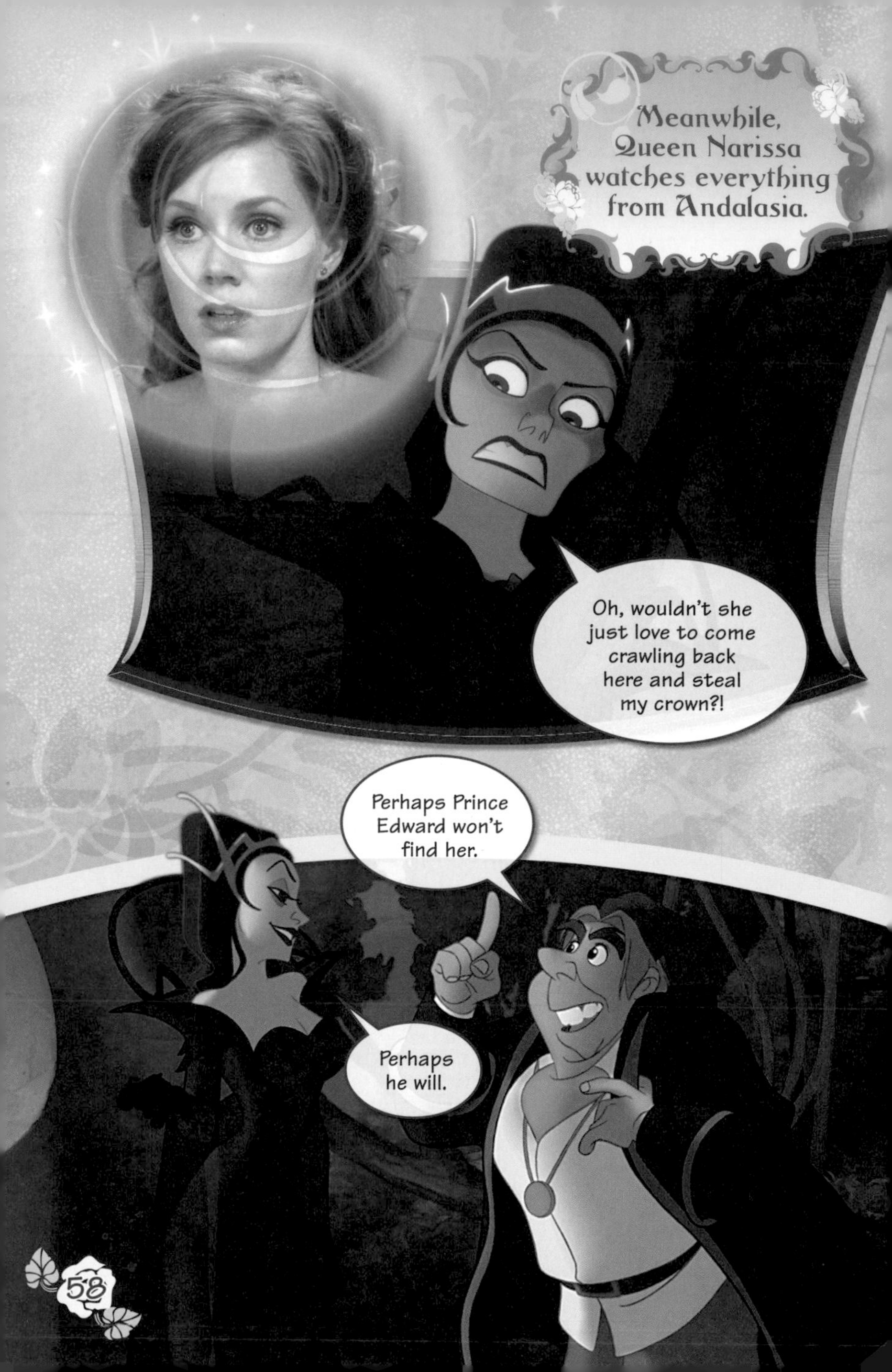
Meanwhile, Queen Narissa watches everything from Andalasia.
Oh, wouldn't she just love to come crawling back here and steal my crown?!
Perhaps Prince Edward won't find her.
Perhaps he will.

The Queen knows she must take action... and who better to help her than Nathaniel.
Oh, I wish there was someone who cared enough for me to go after her.

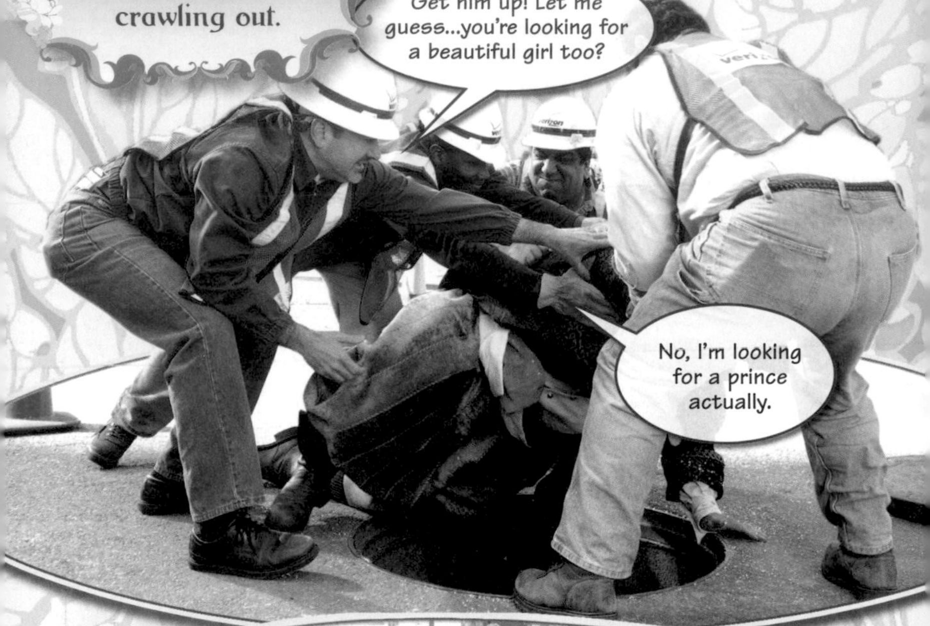
Back at the manhole, something else comes crawling out.
Get him up! Let me guess...you're looking for a beautiful girl too?
No, I'm looking for a prince actually.

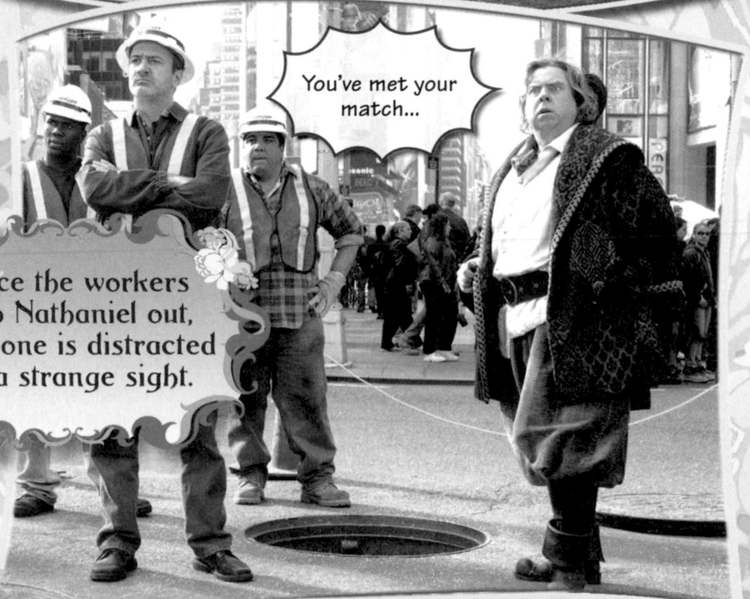
You've met your match...
Once the workers help Nathaniel out, everyone is distracted by a strange sight.

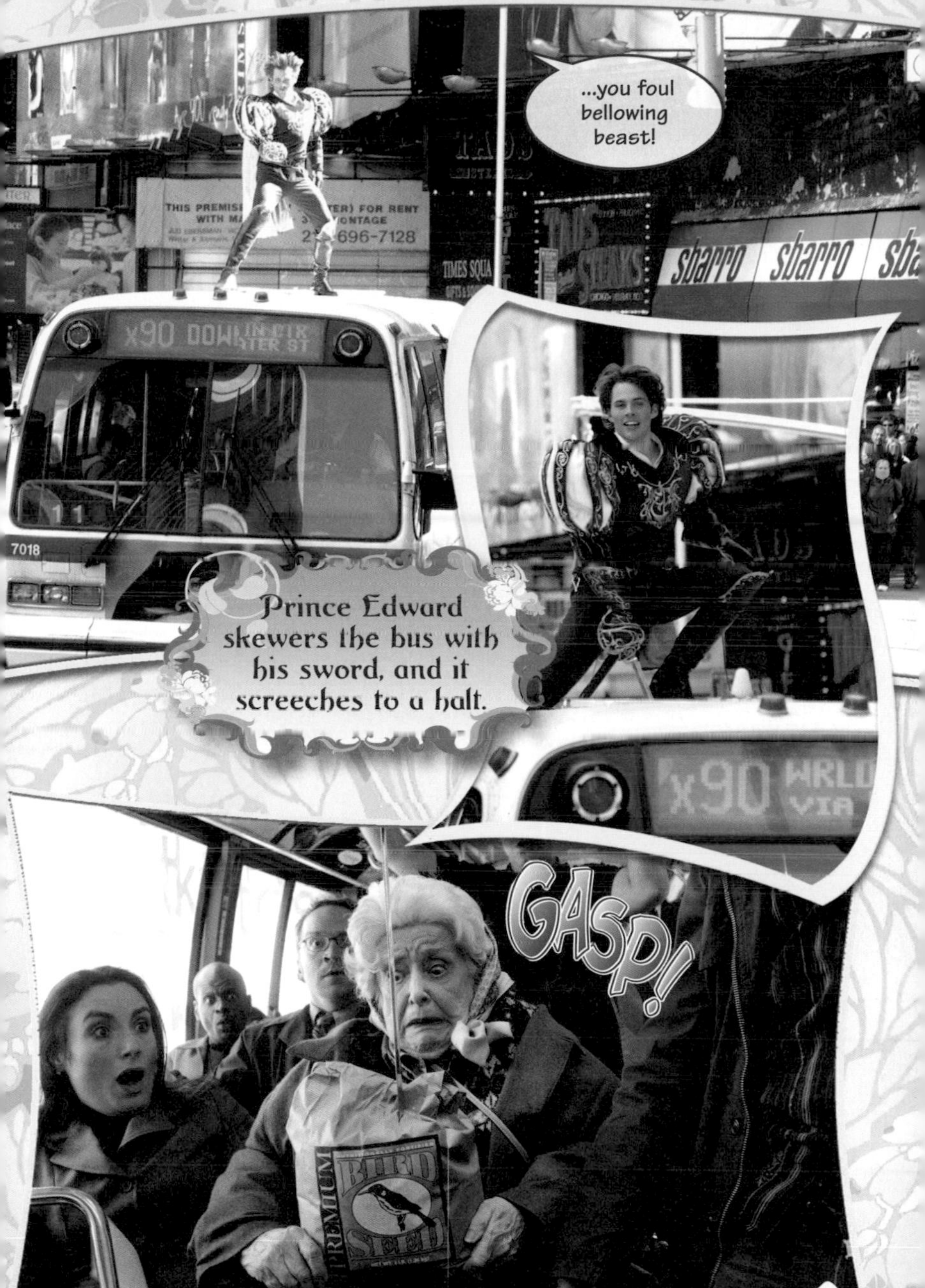
...you foul bellowing beast!
Prince Edward skewers the bus with his sword, and it screeches to a halt.
GASP!

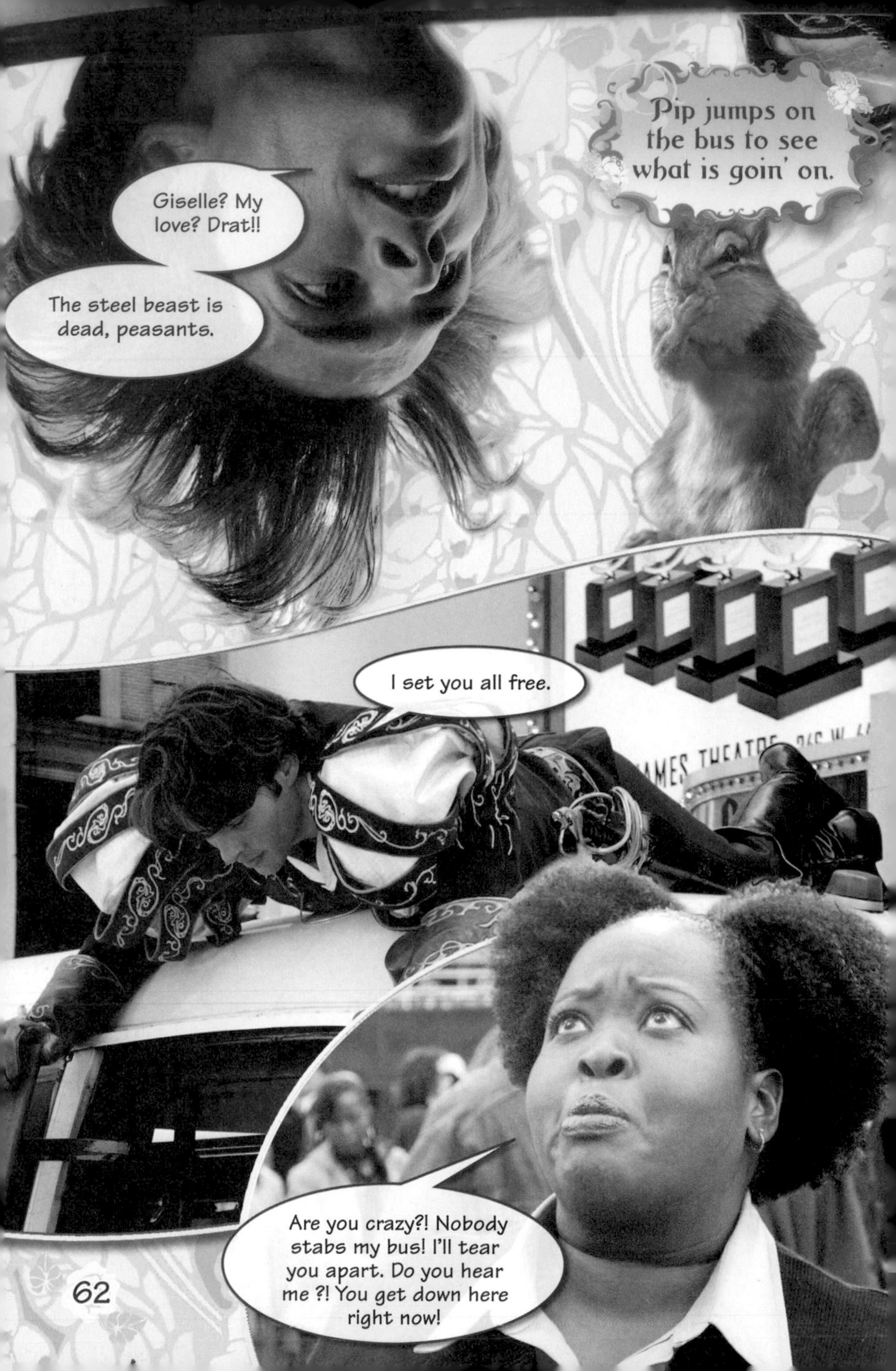
Giselle? My love? Drat!!
The steel beast is dead, peasants.
Pip jumps on the bus to see what is goin' on.
I set you all free.
Are you crazy?! Nobody stabs my bus! I'll tear you apart. Do you hear me ?! You get down here right now!

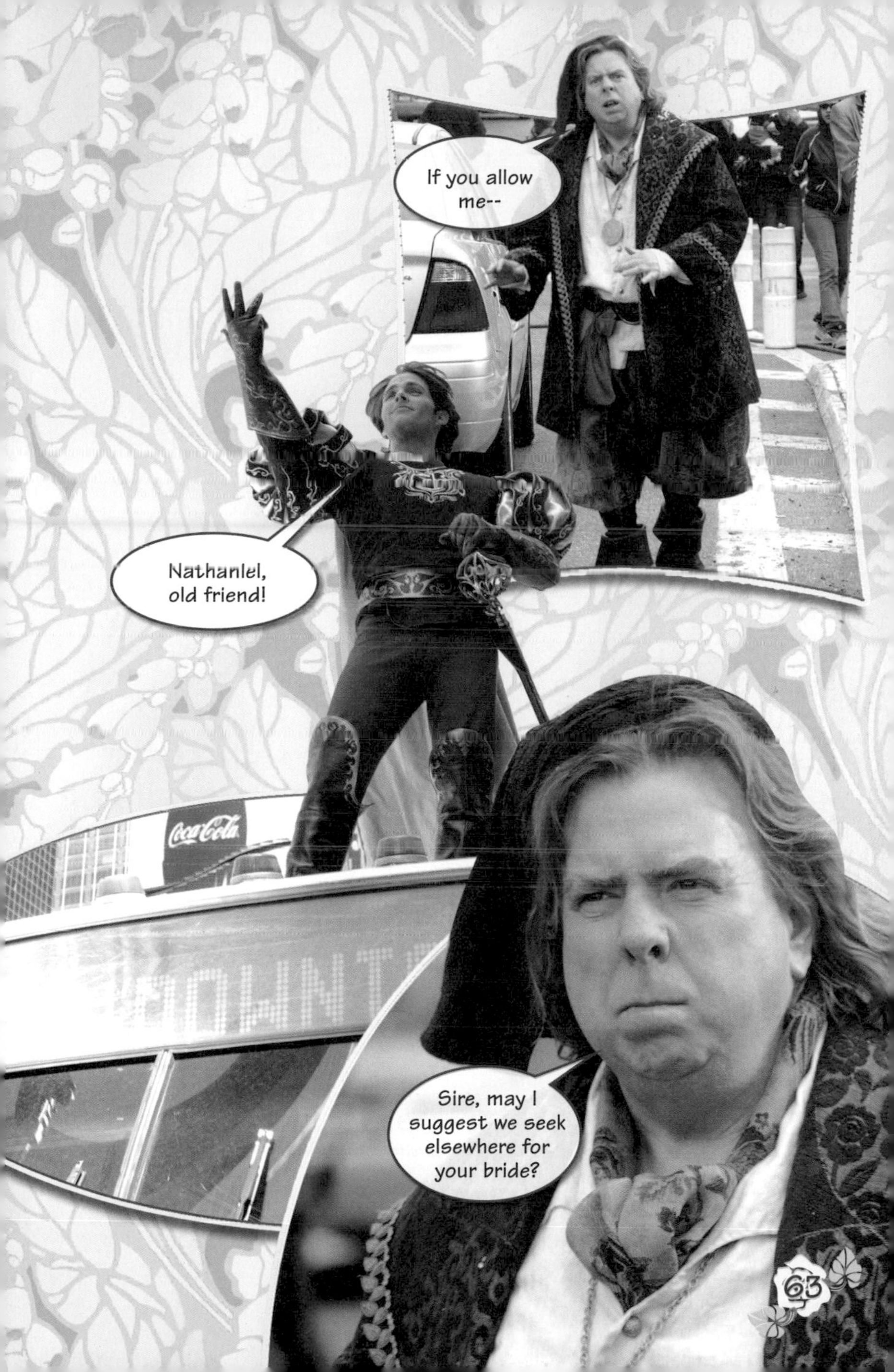
If you allow me--
Nathaniel, old friend!
Sire, may I suggest we seek elsewhere for your bride?

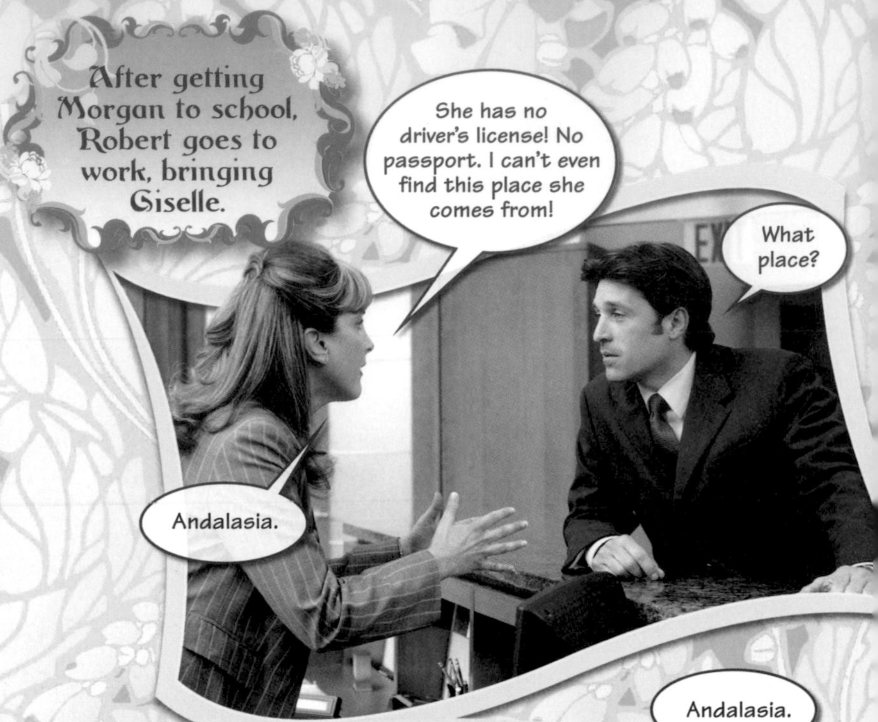
After getting Morgan to school, Robert goes to work, bringing Giselle.
She has no driver's license! No passport. I can't even find this place she comes from!
What place?
Andalasia.

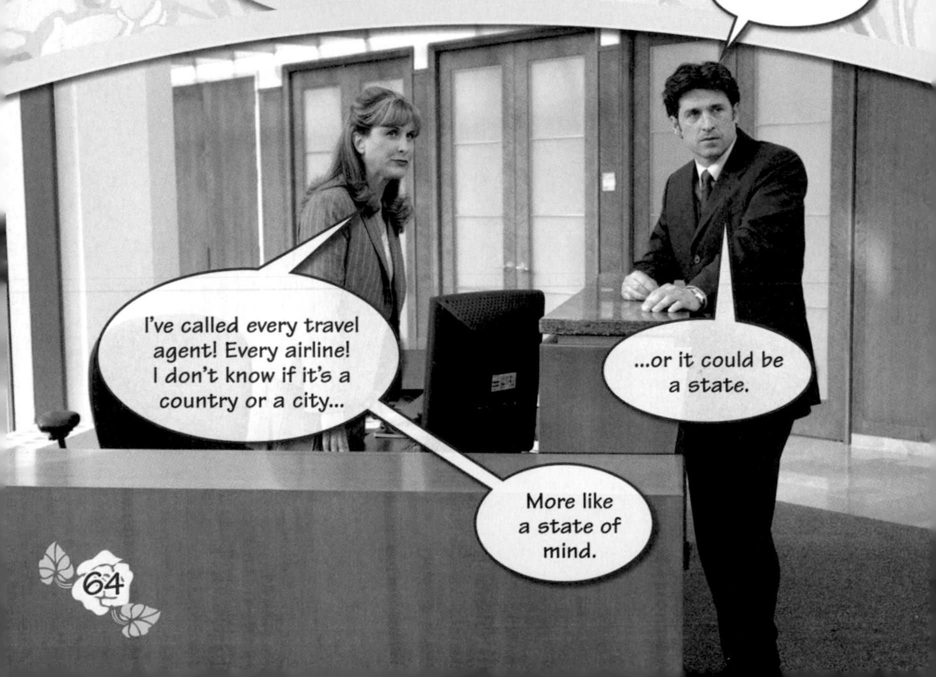
Andalasia.
I've called every travel agent! Every airline! I don't know if it's a country or a city...
...or it could be a state.
More like a state of mind.

With nowhere else to go, Robert takes Giselle to Central Park where they start talking.
So what's the deal with this 'prince' of yours? How long have you been together?
Oh, about a day
You mean it feels like a day? Because you're so in love?
No it's been a day.
You're gonna marry someone after a day? Because you fell in love with him?
Yes, yes.
I don't get it. I mean how can you talk about loving some guy you don't even know?
Well, I know what's in his heart?
Oh. Right. Great.

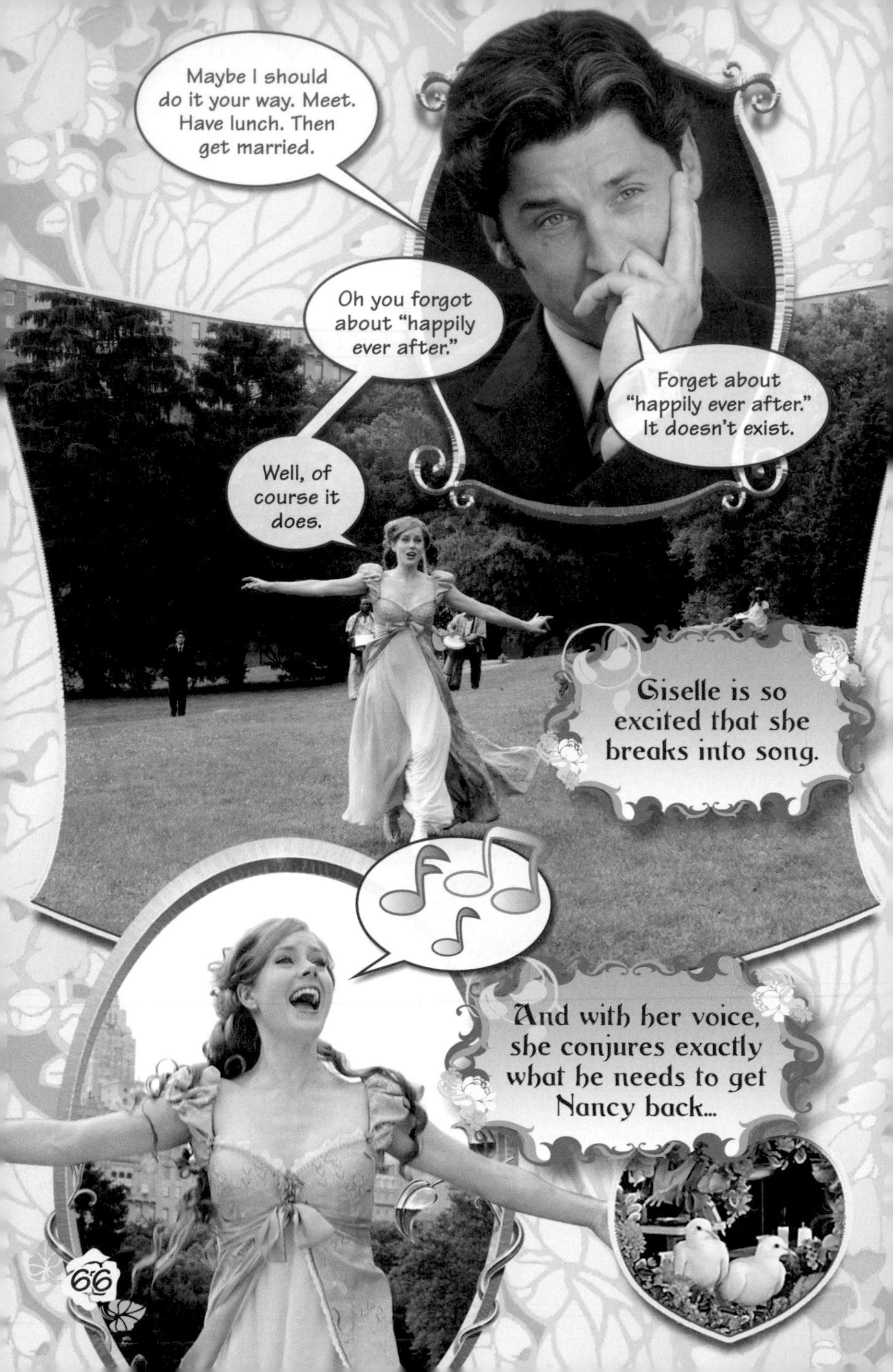
Maybe I should do it your way. Meet. Have lunch. Then get married.
Oh you forgot about "happily ever after."
Forget about "happily ever after." It doesn't exist.
Well, of course it does.
Giselle is so excited that she breaks into song.
And with her voice, she conjures exactly what he needs to get Nancy back...

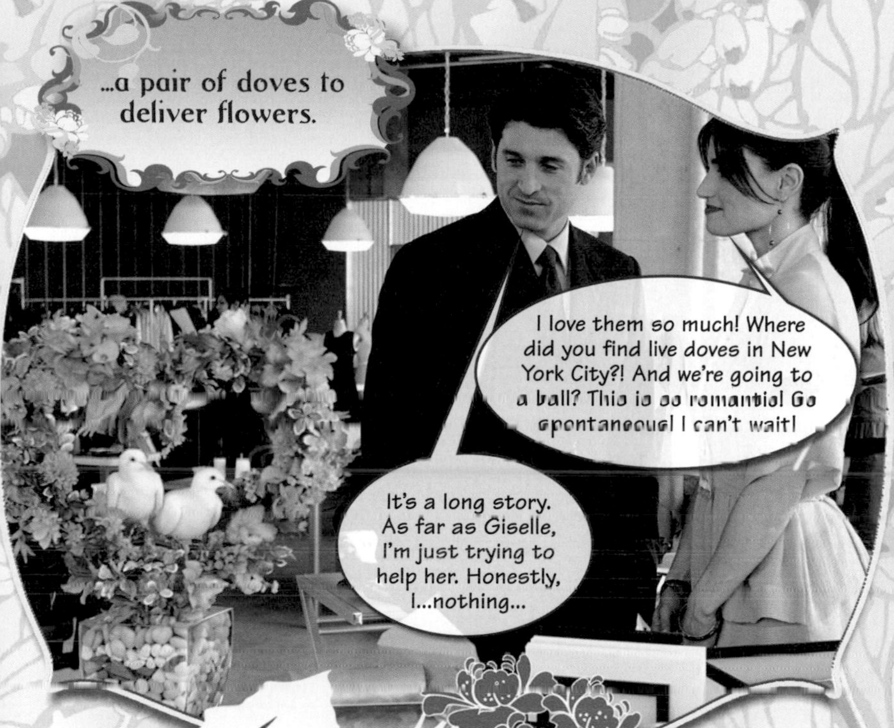
...a pair of doves to deliver flowers.
I love them so much! Where did you find live doves in New York City?! And we're going to a ball? This is so romantic! So spontaneous! I can't wait!
It's a long story. As far as Giselle, I'm just trying to help her. Honestly, I...nothing...

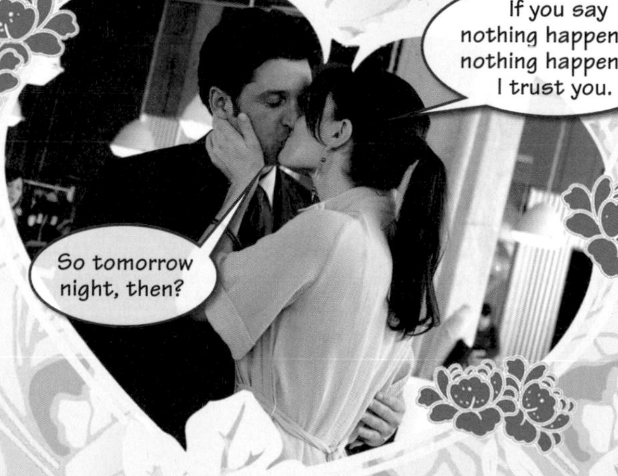
If you say nothing happened, nothing happened. I trust you.
So tomorrow night, then?

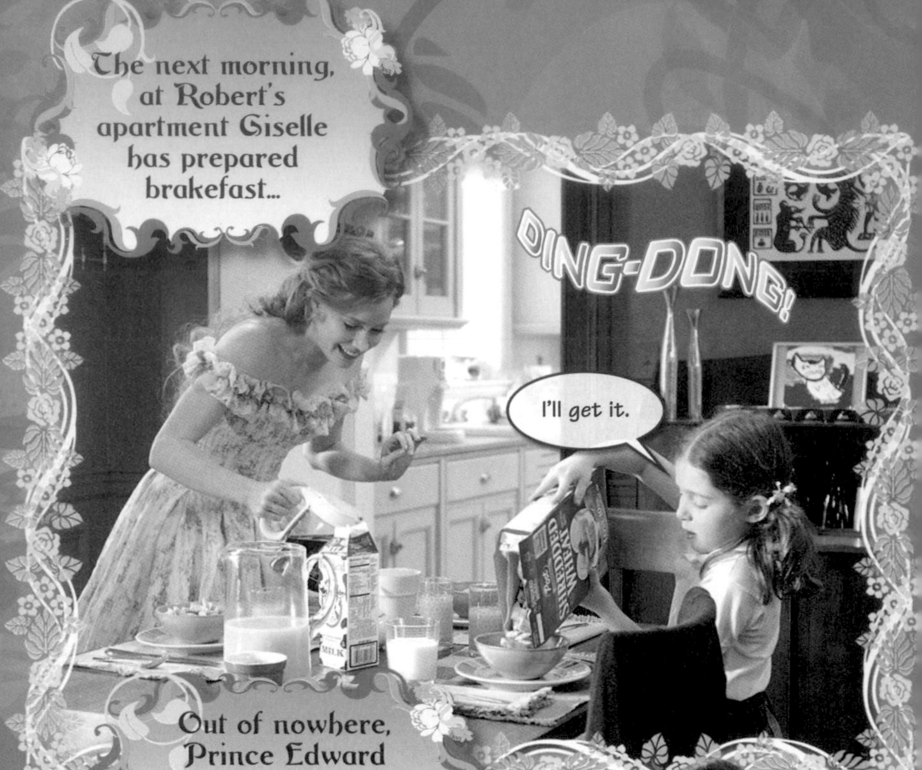
The next morning, at Robert's apartment Giselle has prepared brakefast...
DING-DONG!
I'll get it.

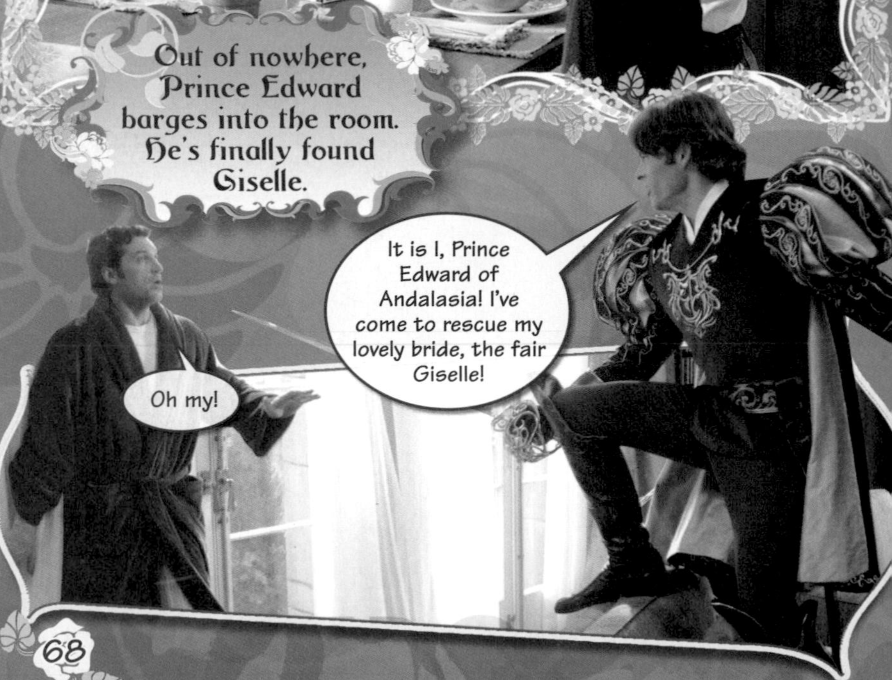
Out of nowhere, Prince Edward barges into the room. He's finally found Giselle.
It is I, Prince Edward of Andalasia! I've come to rescue my lovely bride, the fair Giselle!
Oh my!

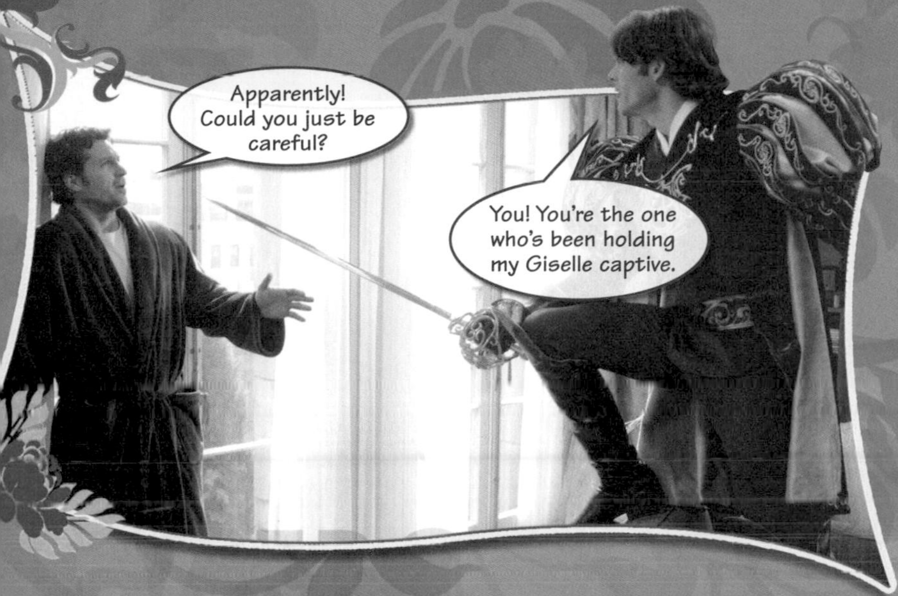
Apparently! Could you just be careful?
You! You're the one who's been holding my Giselle captive.

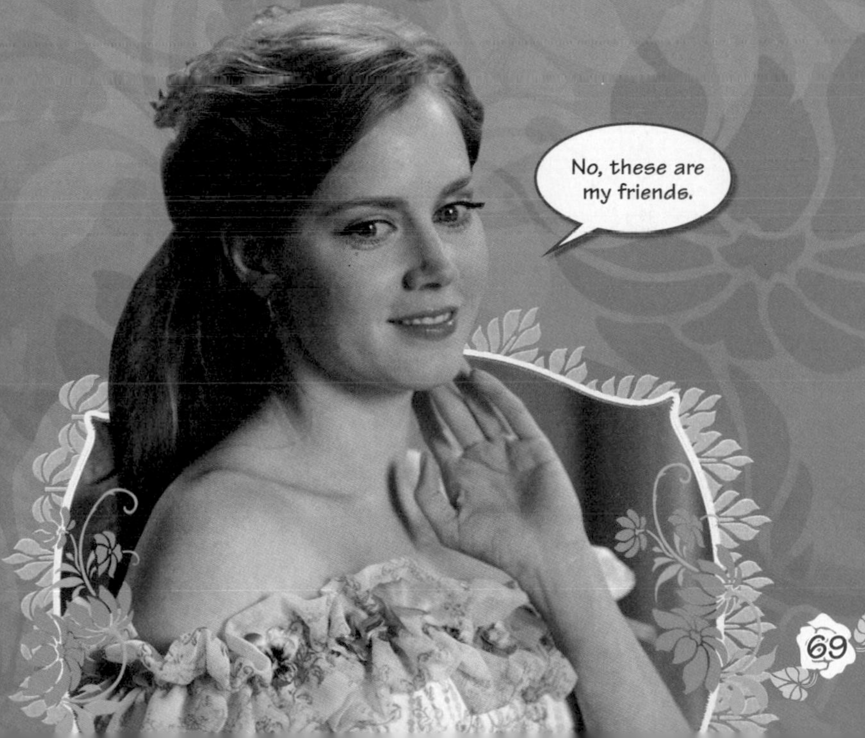
No, these are my friends.

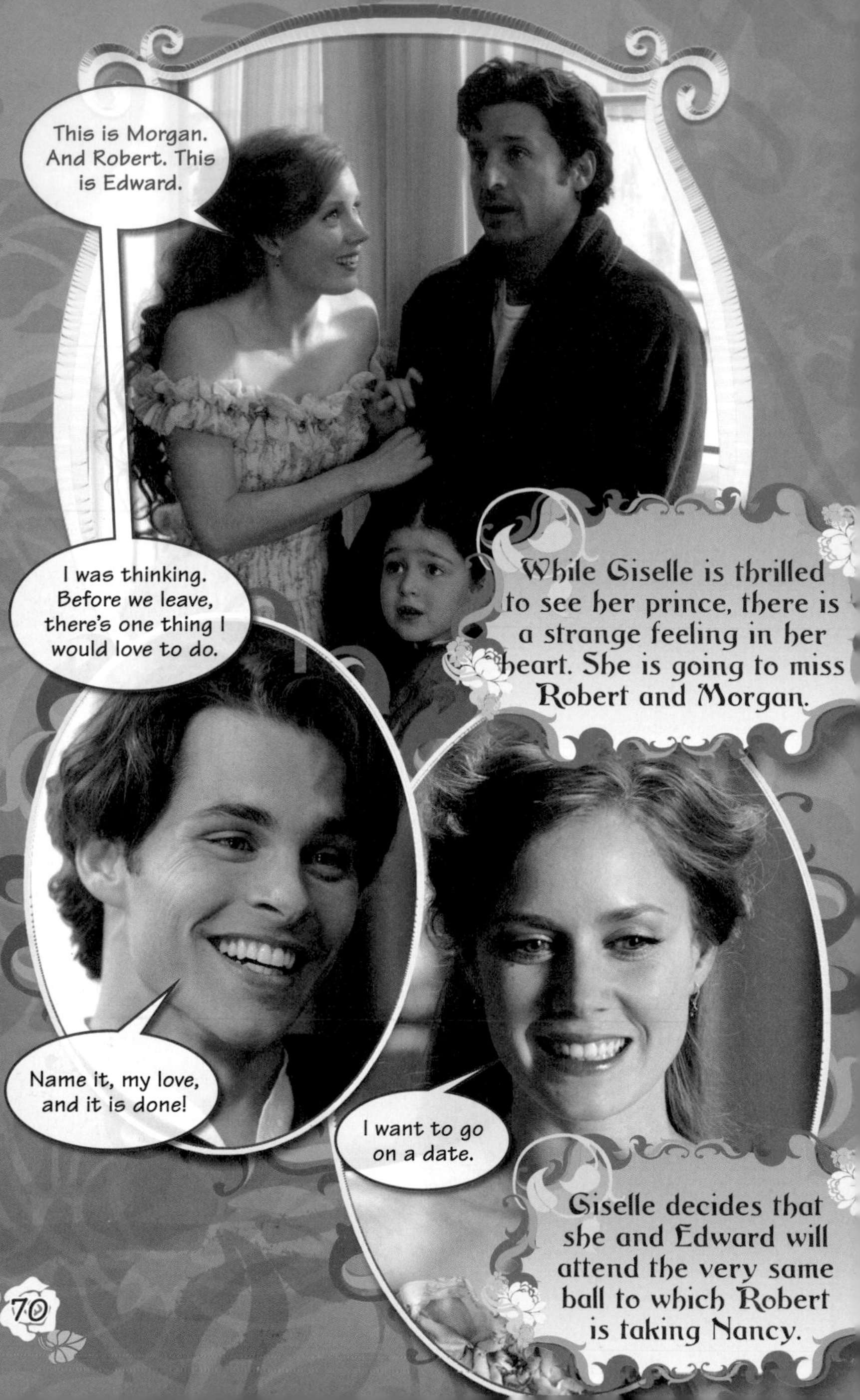
This is Morgan. And Robert. This is Edward.
I was thinking. Before we leave, there's one thing I would love to do.
While Giselle is thrilled to see her prince, there is a strange feeling in her heart. She is going to miss Robert and Morgan.
Name it, my love, and it is done!
I want to go on a date.
Giselle decides that she and Edward will attend the very same ball to which Robert is taking Nancy.

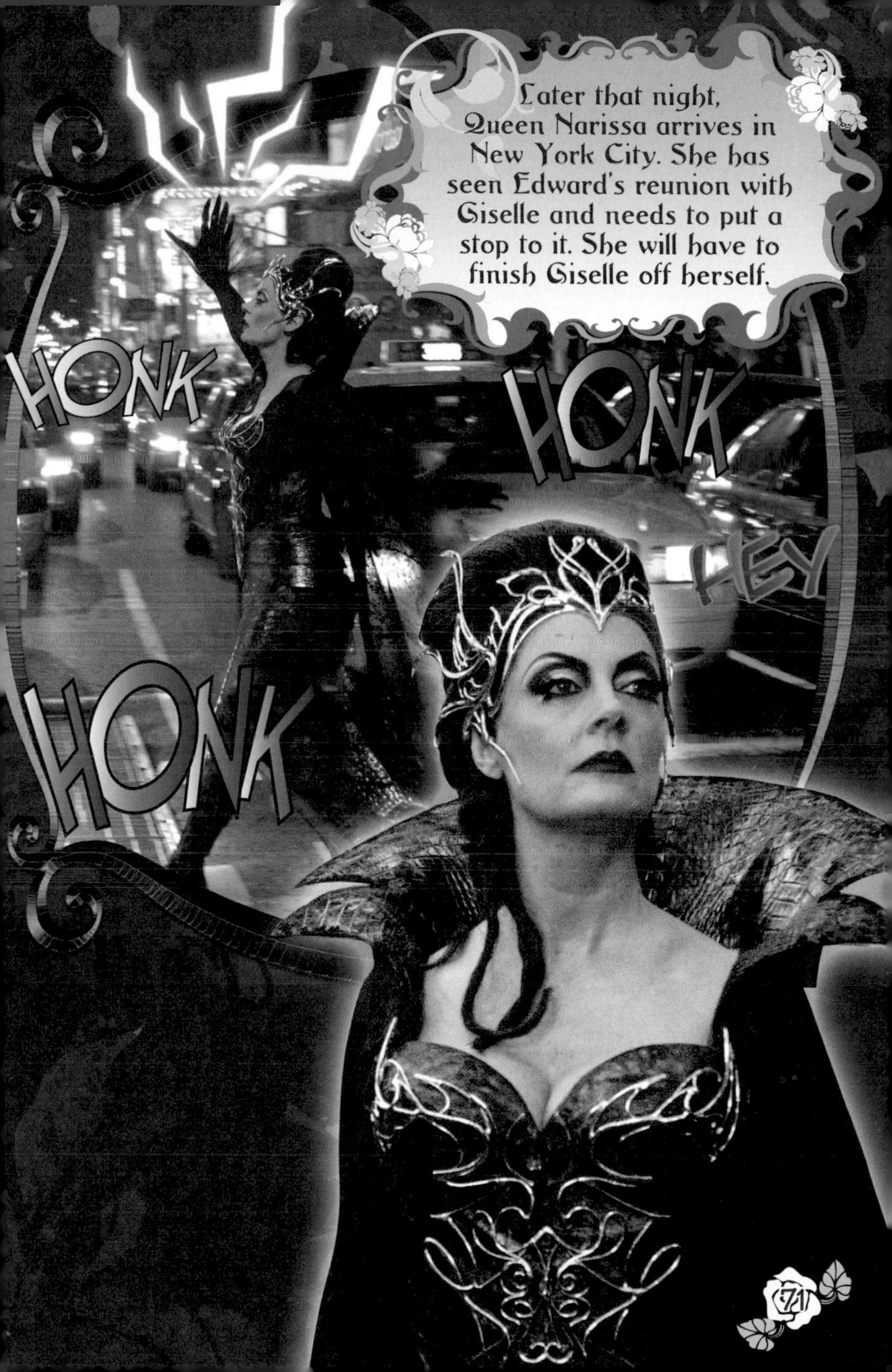
Later that night, Queen Narissa arrives in New York City. She has seen Edward's reunion with Giselle and needs to put a stop to it. She will have to finish Giselle off herself.
HONK
HONK
HEY
HONK

At the ball, Robert and Nancy try to rekindle their love.

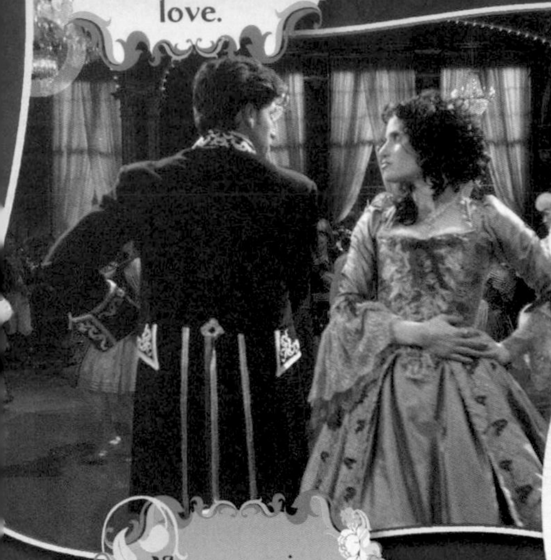

Prince Edward escorts Giselle, who looks beautiful in her new dress.

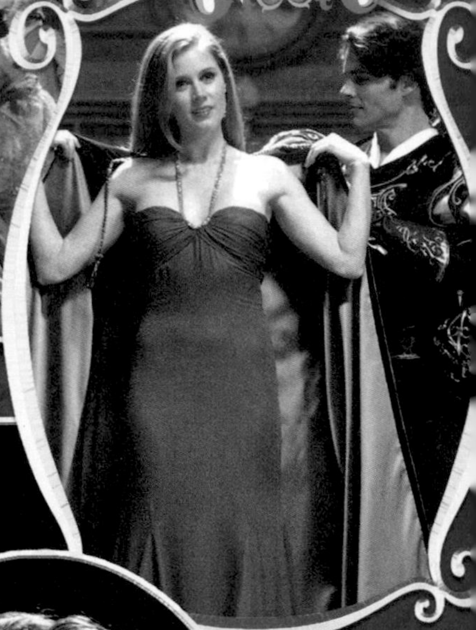

Upon seeing Giselle, Robert asks her to dance and...

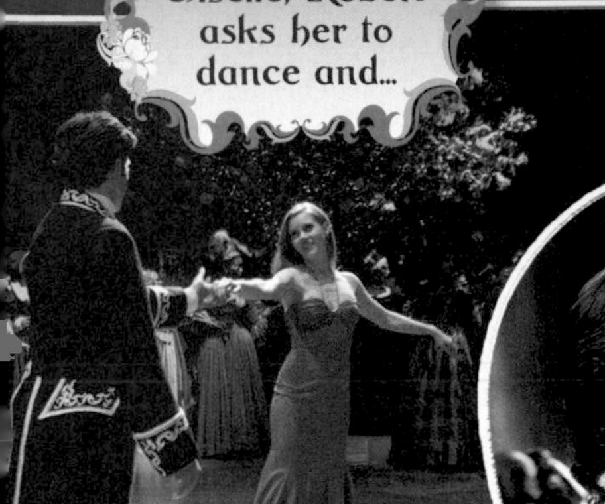

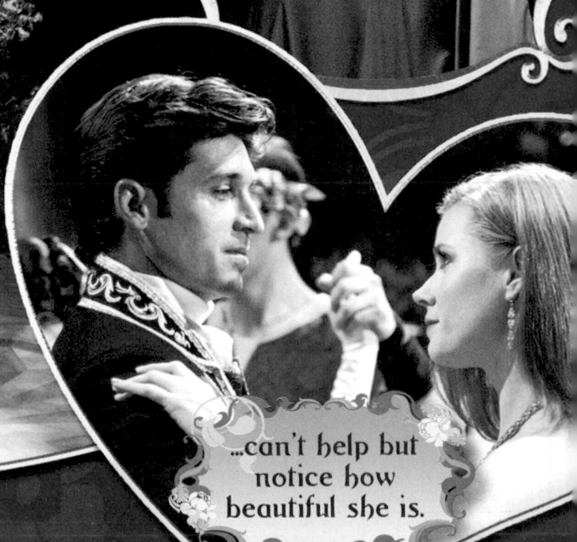

...can't help but notice how beautiful she is.

But the mood is quickly ruined as Giselle recognizes the Old Hag from Andalasia.
You! You sent me here!
I'm so glad to see you, child. I've been so very worried.
Such a terrible accident that brought you to this terrible place! Just one bite and all this will go away. You won't remember anything!
Looking down at the dance floor, Giselle sees Robert and Nancy dancing. It breaks her heart!
MUNCH
She loves Robert but knows she can never be with him. With a sigh, she takes a bite of the apple and falls to the floor, unconcious.

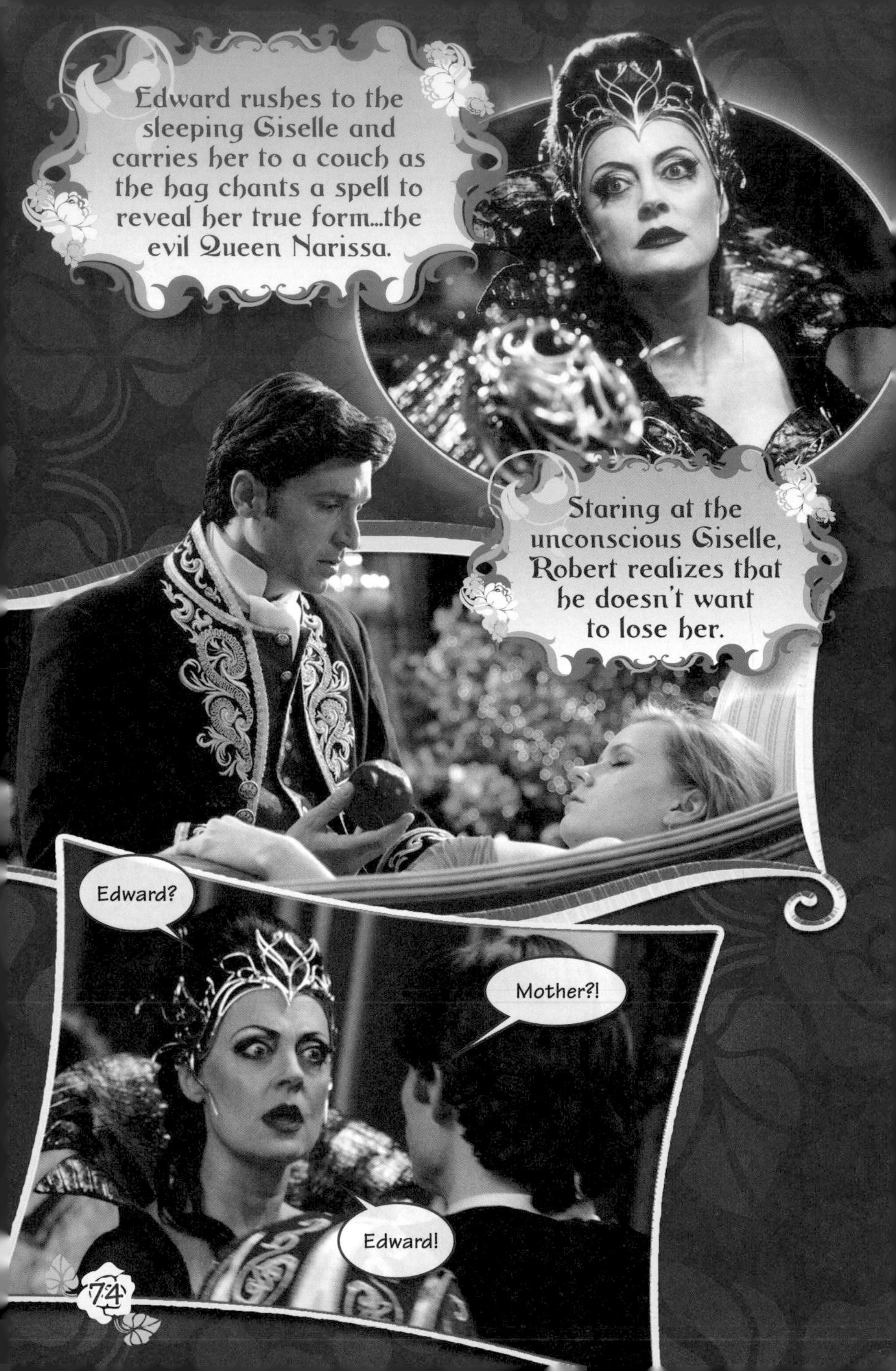
Edward rushes to the sleeping Giselle and carries her to a couch as the hag chants a spell to reveal her true form...the evil Queen Narissa.
Staring at the unconscious Giselle, Robert realizes that he doesn't want to lose her.
Edward?
Mother?!
Edward!

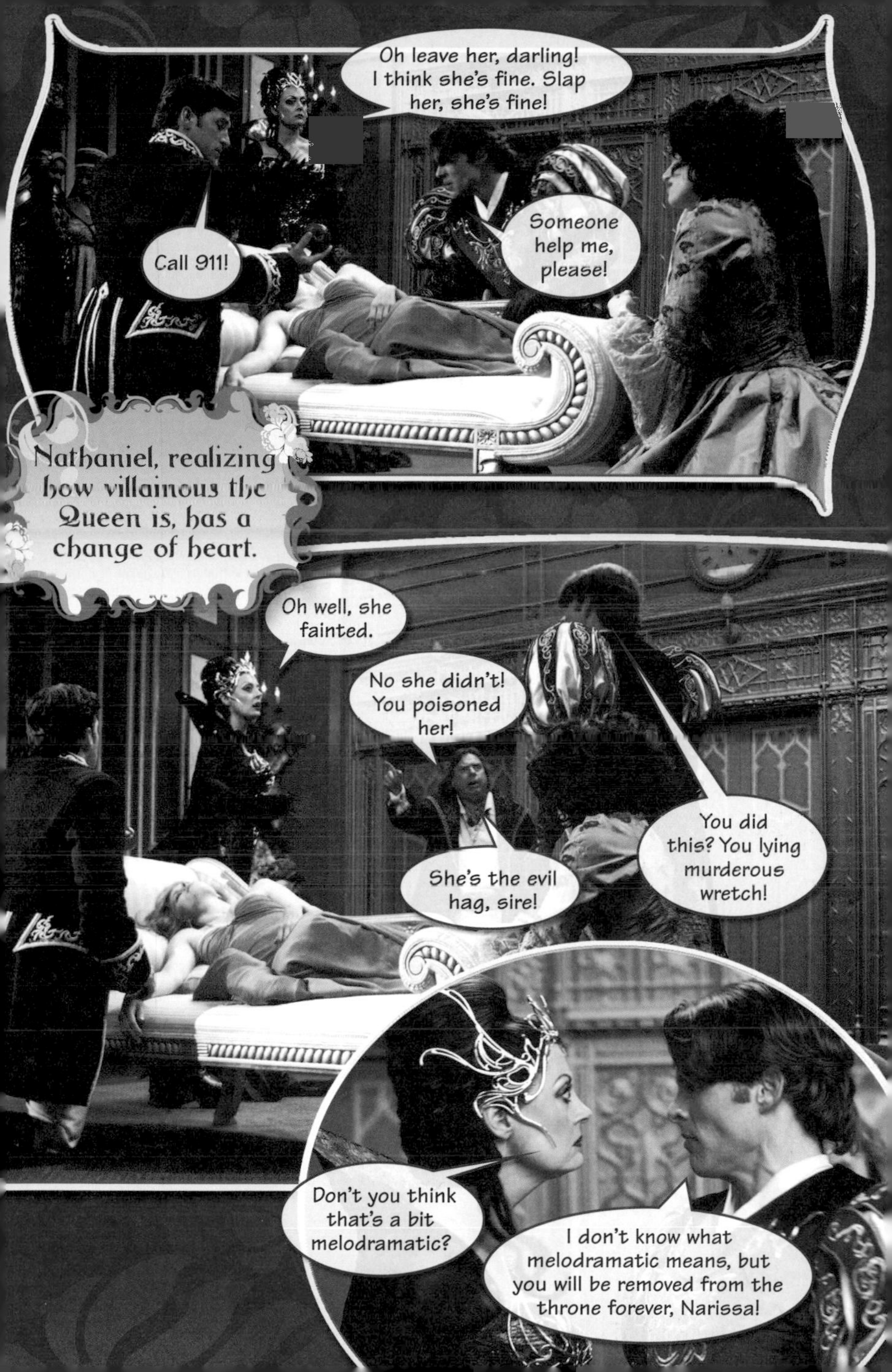
Oh leave her, darling! I think she's fine. Slap her, she's fine!
Call 911!
Someone help me, please!
Nathaniel, realizing how villainous the Queen is, has a change of heart.
Oh well, she fainted.
No she didn't! You poisoned her!
She's the evil hag, sire!
You did this? You lying murderous wretch!
Don't you think that's a bit melodramatic?
I don't know what melodramatic means, but you will be removed from the throne forever, Narissa!

Nathaniel grabs Edward's sword and convinces the queen to remain silent.
That's enough from you, you viper!
DONG!
We have to help her. What can we do?
DONG!
You'll never save her now! When the clock strikes twelve, she'll be dead!
DONG!
True love's kiss? It is the most powerful thing in the world!
Prince Edward kisses Giselle but nothing happens.
DONG!
Edward steps aside to allow Robert a try.

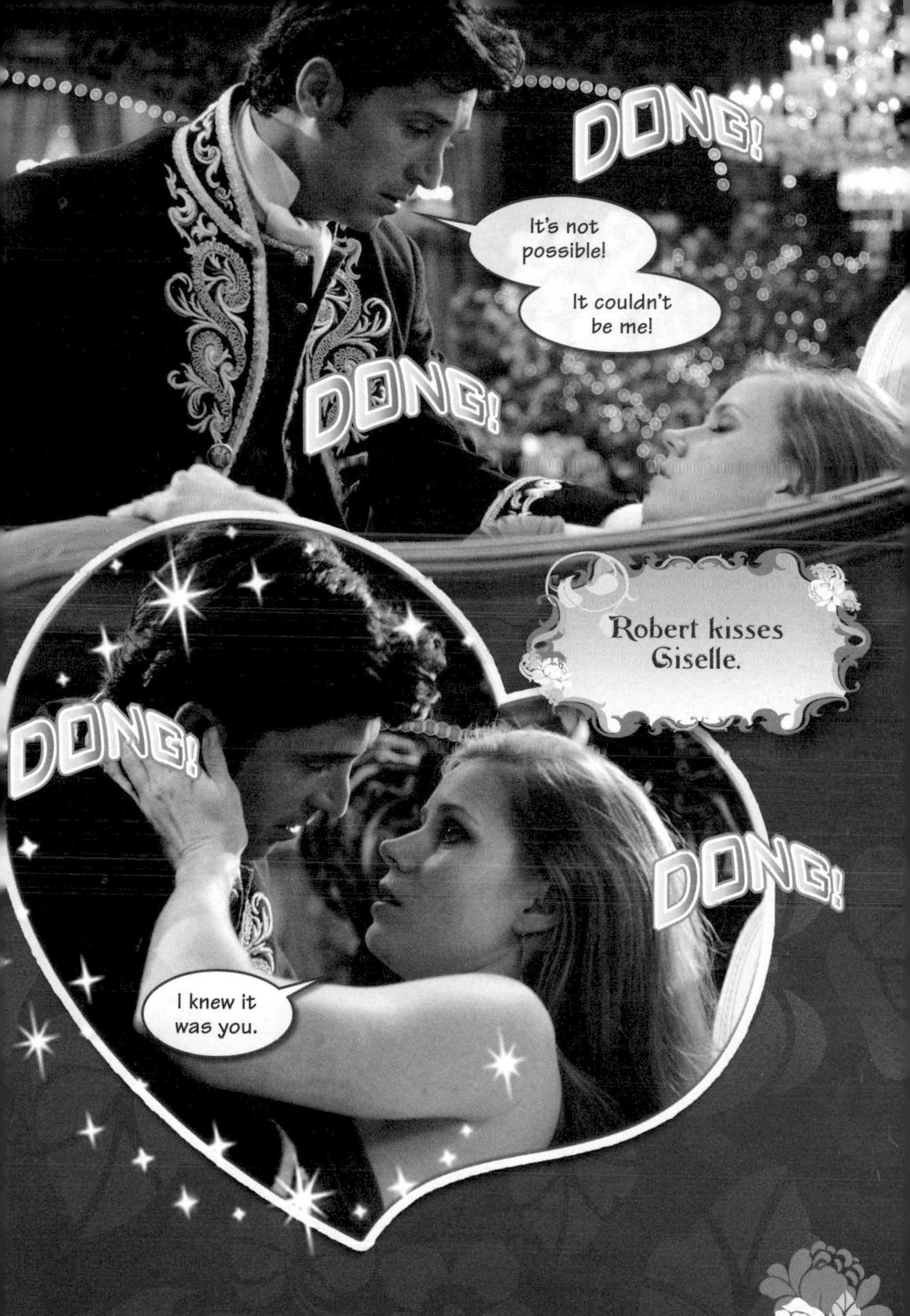
DONG!
It's not possible!
It couldn't be me!
DONG!
Robert kisses Giselle.
DONG!
DONG!
I knew it was you.

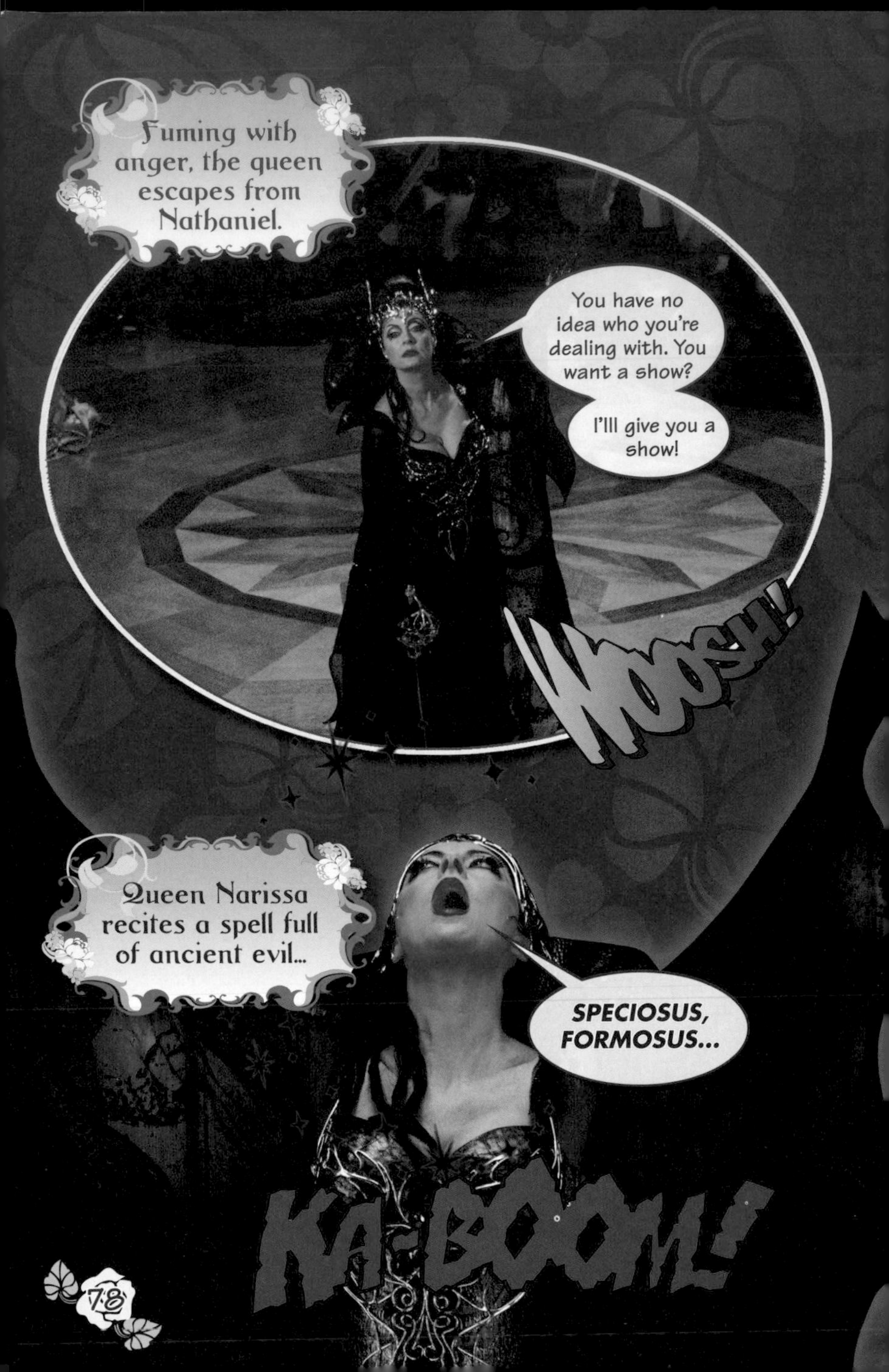
Fuming with anger, the queen escapes from Nathaniel.
You have no idea who you're dealing with. You want a show?
I'll give you a show!
WOOSH!
Queen Narissa recites a spell full of ancient evil...
SPECIOSUS, FORMOSUS...
KA-BOOM!

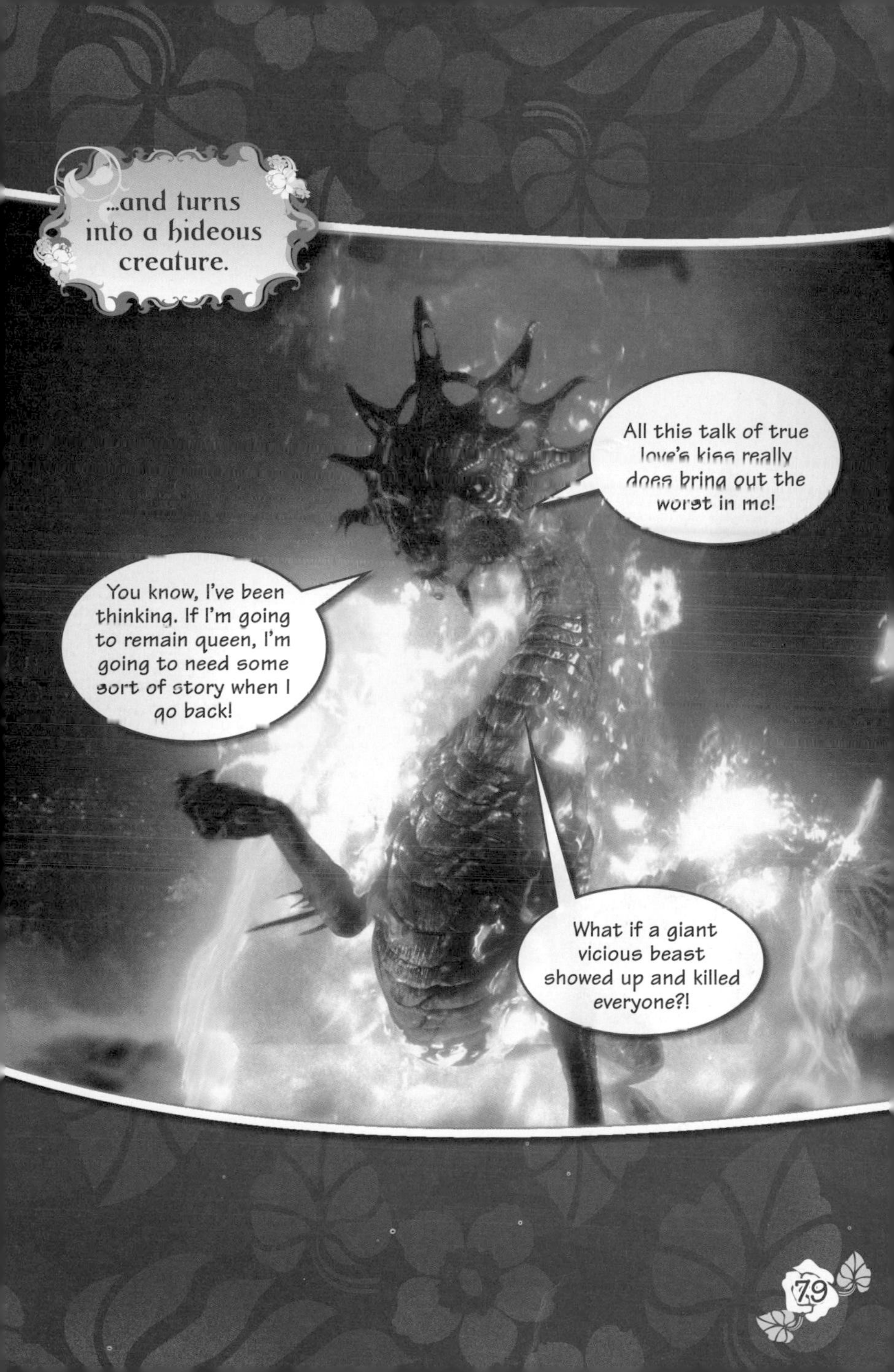
...and turns into a hideous creature.
All this talk of true love's kiss really does bring out the worst in me!
You know, I've been thinking. If I'm going to remain queen, I'm going to need some sort of story when I go back!
What if a giant vicious beast showed up and killed everyone?!

Queen Narissa grabs Robert and climbs outside the building with him in her claws.
Let me go! Put me down! You're crazy!
No! Spiteful, vindictive, very large...but never crazy!

Narissa, I'm not going to let you take him!
Giselle, armed with Edward's sword, climbs out after the Queen to save Robert.

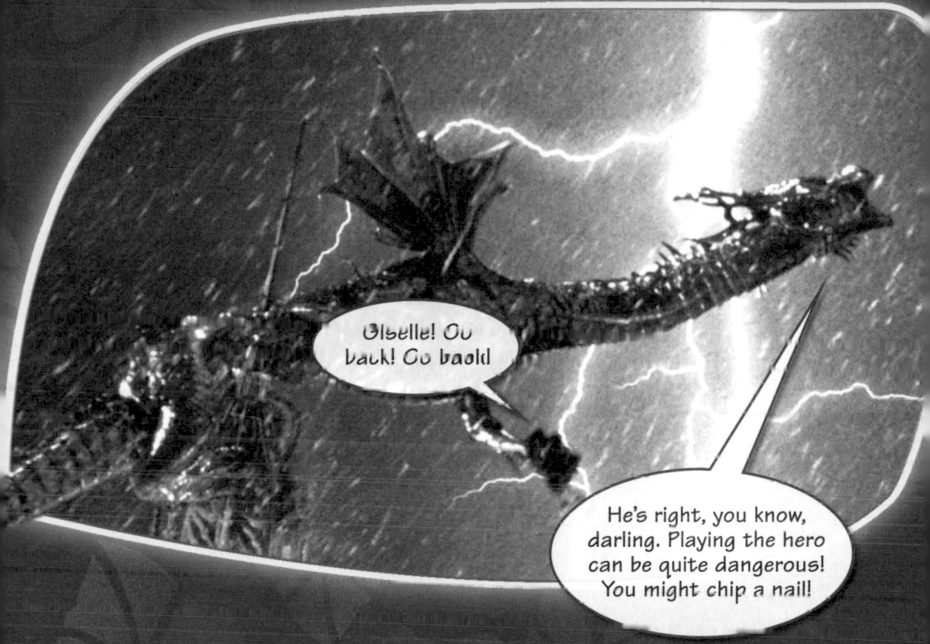
Giselle! Go back! Go back!
He's right, you know, darling. Playing the hero can be quite dangerous! You might chip a nail!

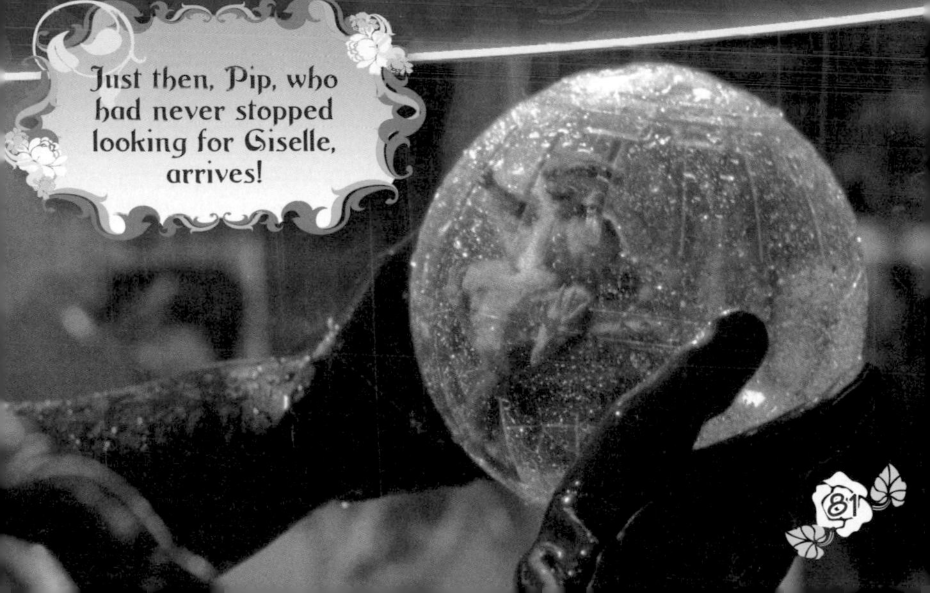
Just then, Pip, who had never stopped looking for Giselle, arrives!

We're coming to the end of our tale now...
...I'm just dying to know how it ends!
ROOOOOOAAARRRR!
Pip jumps on the Queen Narissa's head as Giselle hurls Prince Edward's sword at the beast.
CRASH!
The sword narrowly misses the Queen, but catches Robert's shirt, pinning him to the building. Pip's added weight causes the roof to give way sending Queen Narissa falling to her death!

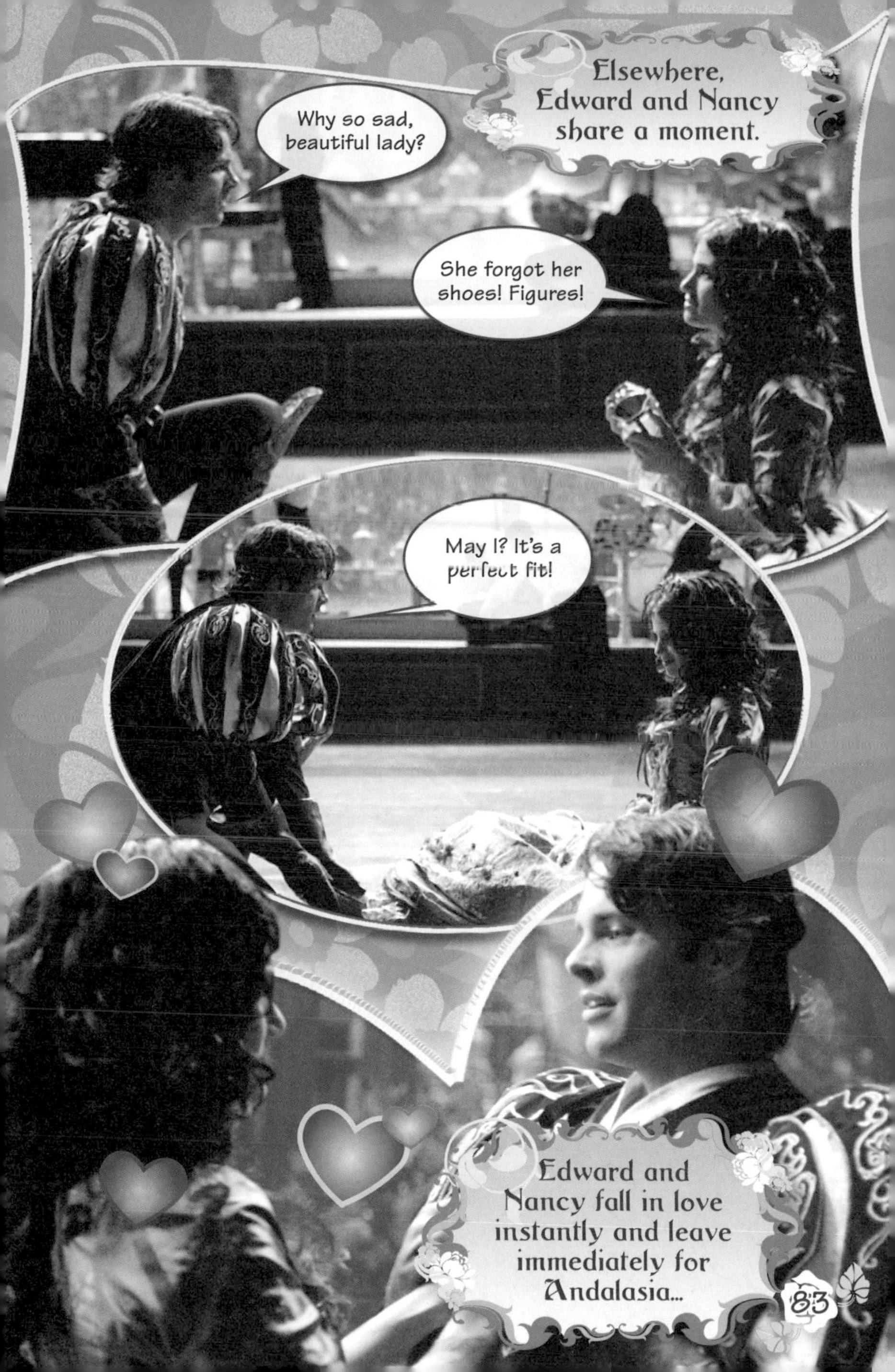
Elsewhere, Edward and Nancy share a moment.
Why so sad, beautiful lady?
She forgot her shoes! Figures!
May I? It's a perfect fit!
Edward and Nancy fall in love instantly and leave immediately for Andalasia...

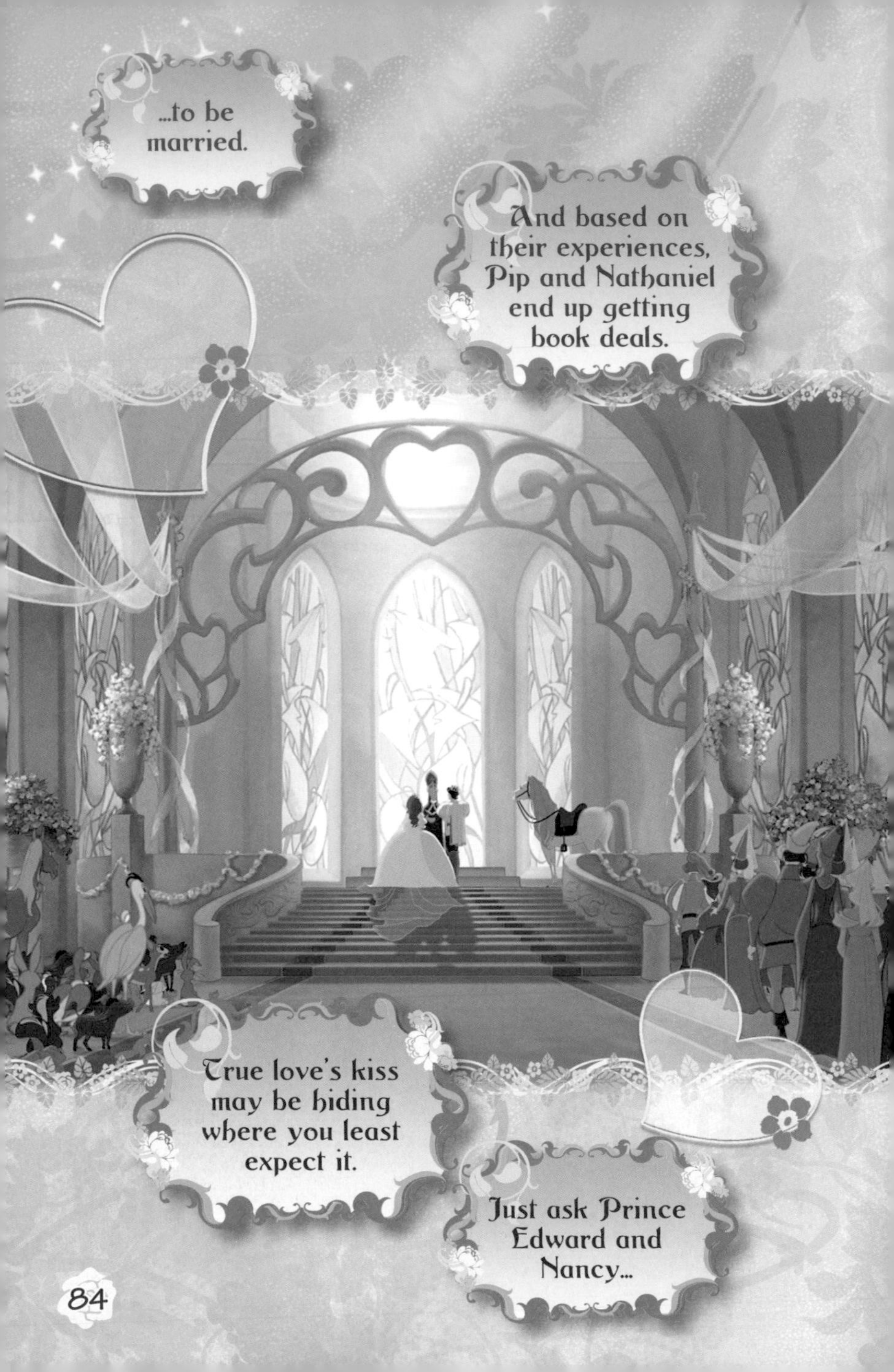
...to be married.
And based on their experiences, Pip and Nathaniel end up getting book deals.
True love's kiss may be hiding where you least expect it.
Just ask Prince Edward and Nancy...

...or Giselle and Robert.

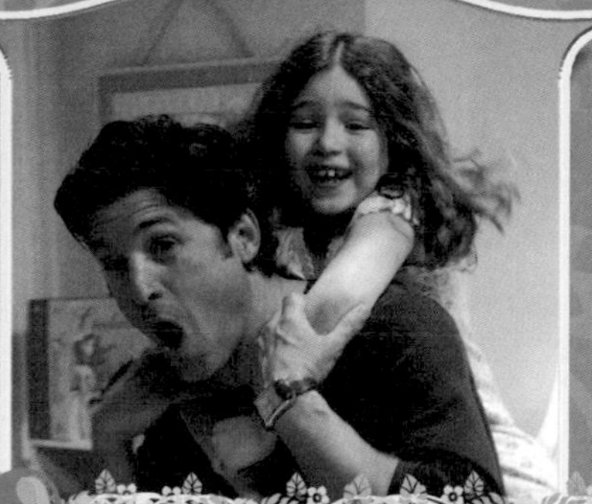

You never know where true love's kiss will find you... but it will.

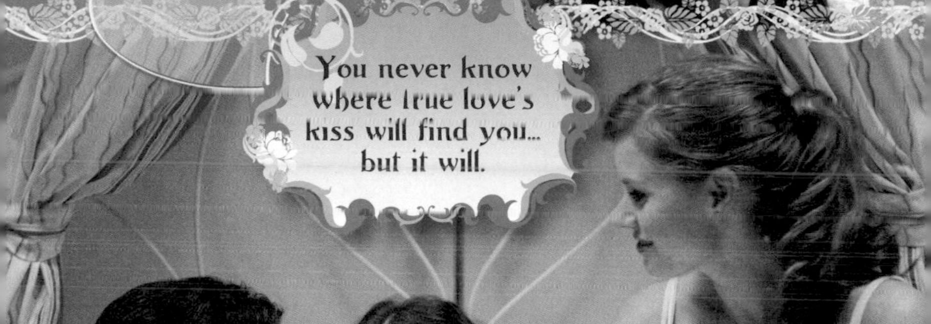

And so... They all lived happily ever after.

The End!

Enchanted Visual Development for the animated scenes

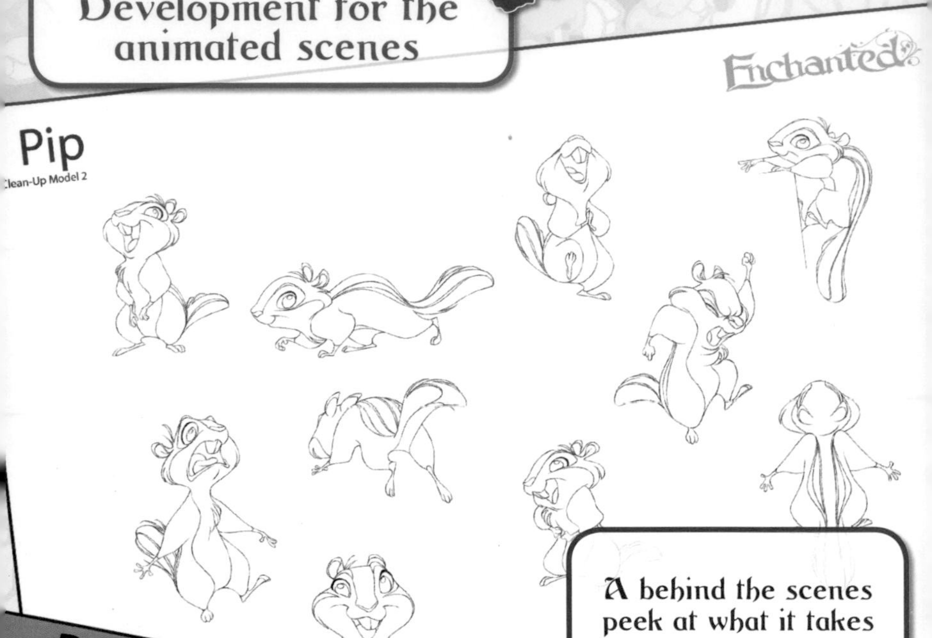
Enchanted
Pip
Clean-Up Model 2

A behind the scenes peek at what it takes to complete the animated section of Enchanted...

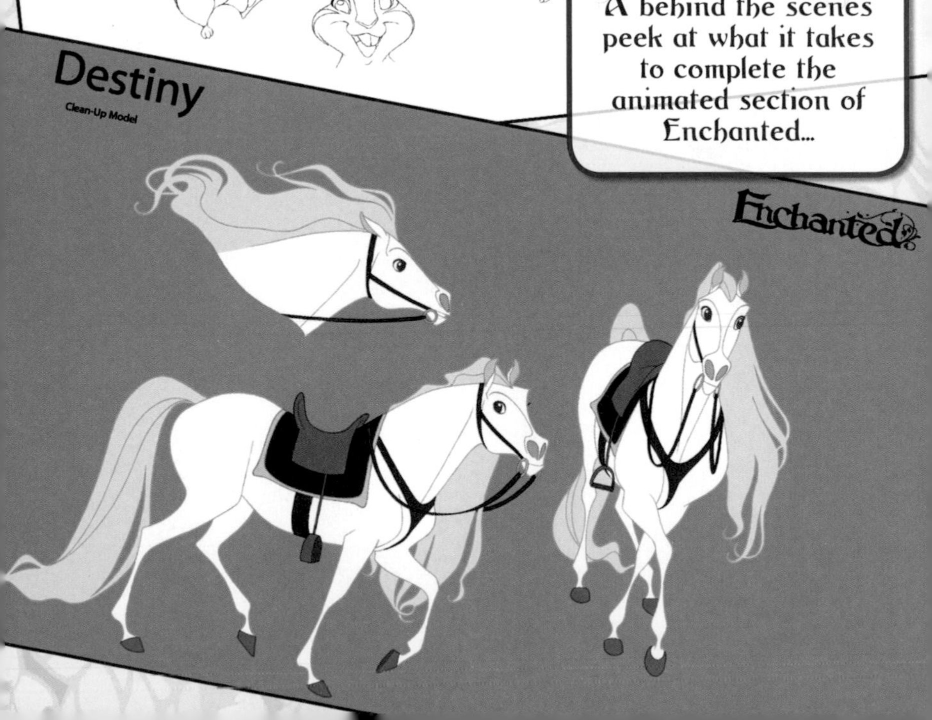
Destiny
Clean-Up Model
Enchanted

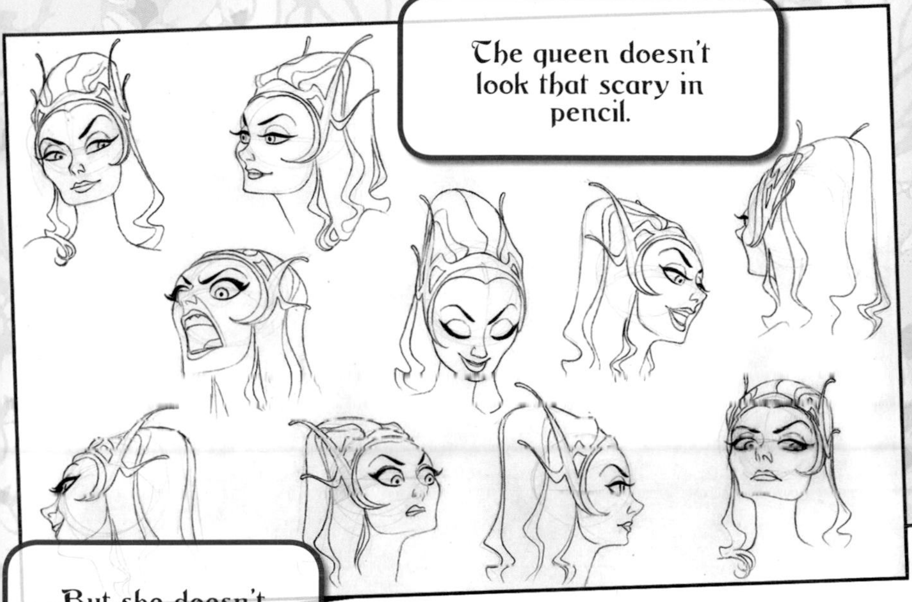
The queen doesn't look that scary in pencil.

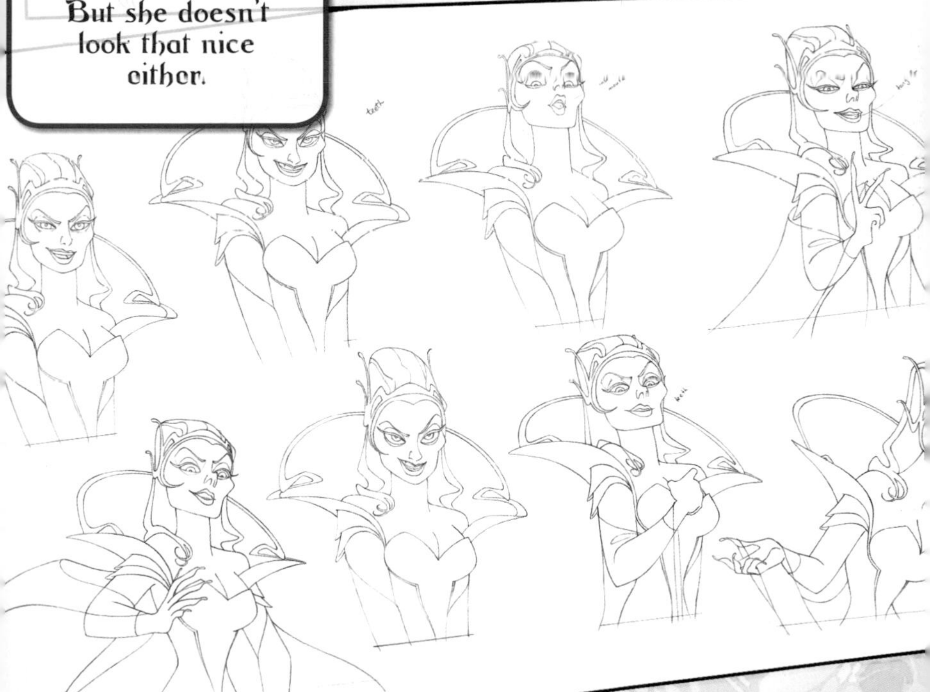
But she doesn't look that nice either.

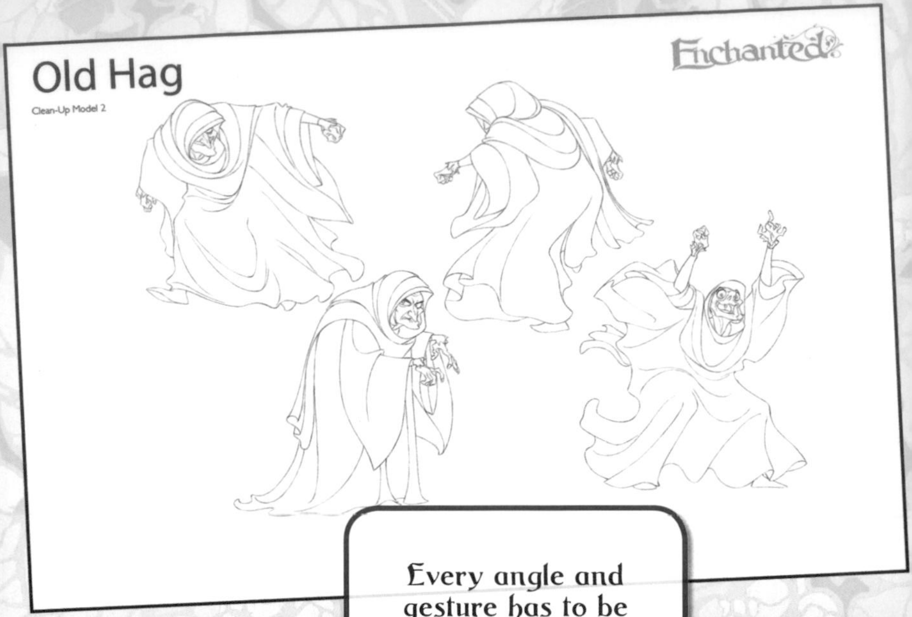
Old Hag
Clean-Up Model 2
Enchanted

Every angle and gesture has to be panned out before the animators can start animating the movie.

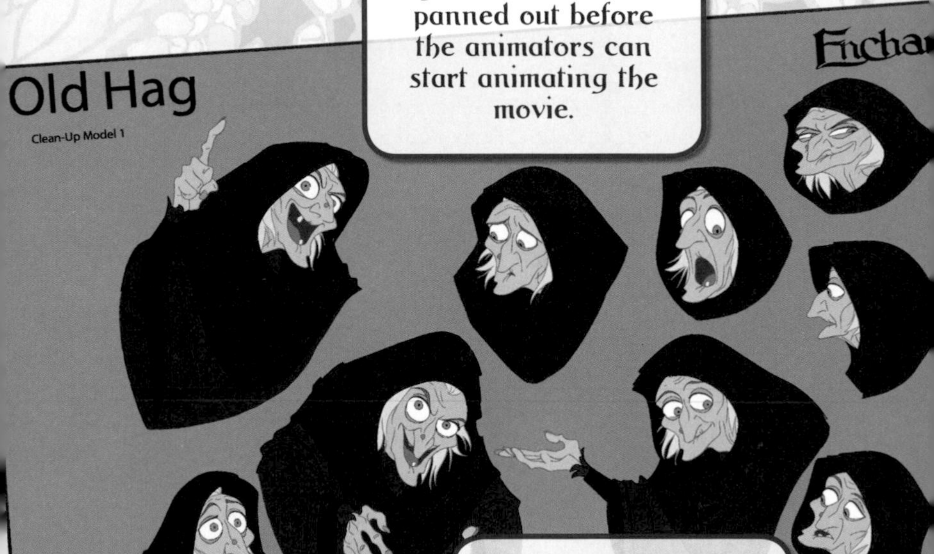
Old Hag
Clean-Up Model 1

Every color has to be figured out, too!

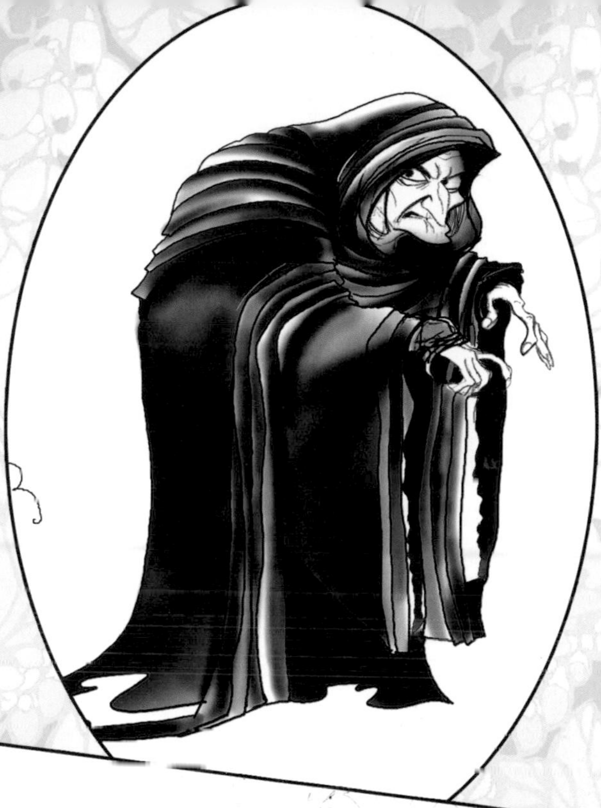

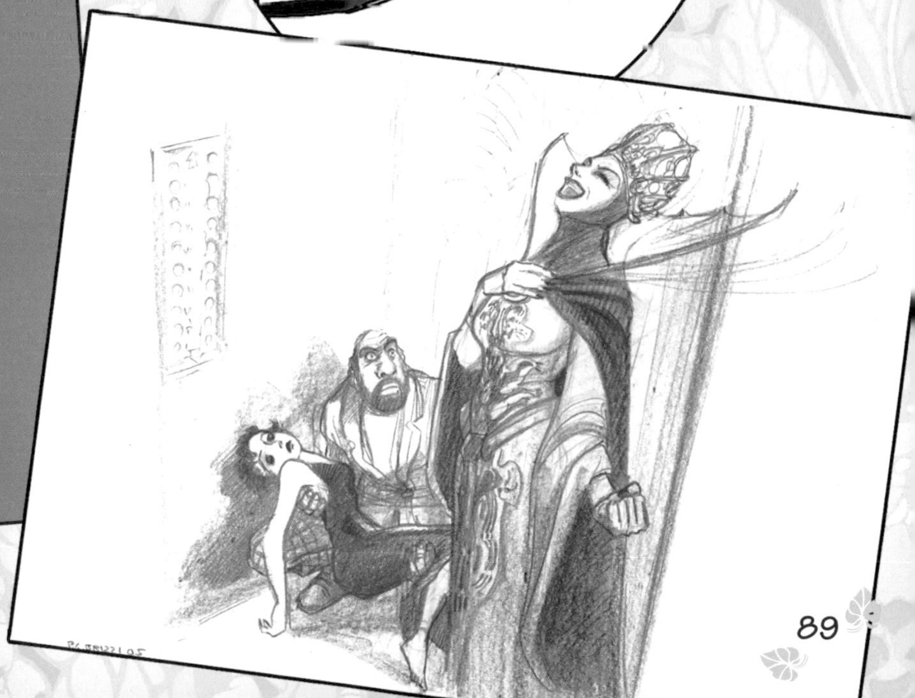

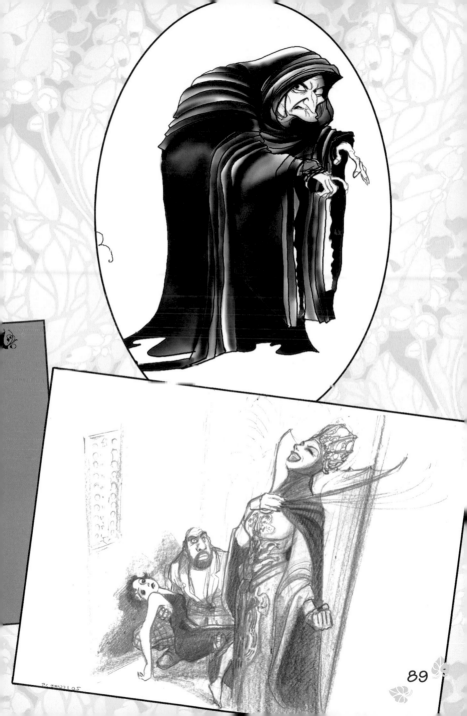

Experience your favorite movies and TV shows in the palm of your hand...

...with TOKYOPOP® CINE-MANGA® books!

- Aladdin
- All Grown Up
- The Amanda Show
- Avatar
- Bambi
- Barbie™ as the Princess and the Pauper
- Barbie™ Fairytopia
- Barbie™ of Swan Lake
- Chicken Little
- Cinderella
- Drake & Josh
- Duel Masters
- The Fairly OddParents
- Finding Nemo
- Future Greatest Stars of the NBA: LeBron James, Dwyane Wade and Carmelo Anthony
- G.I. Joe Spy Troops
- Greatest Stars of the NBA: Tim Duncan
- Greatest Stars of the NBA: Kevin Garnett
- Greatest Stars of the NBA: Allen Iverson
- Greatest Stars of the NBA: Jason Kidd
- Greatest Stars of the NBA: Shaquille O'Neal
- The Incredibles
- The Adventures of Jimmy Neutron: Boy Genius
- Kim Possible
- Lilo & Stitch: The Series
- Lizzie McGuire
- Madagascar
- Mucha Lucha!
- Pooh's Heffalump Movie
- Power Rangers
- The Princess Diaries 2
- Rave Master
- Romeo!
- Shrek 2
- SpongeBob SquarePants
- Spy Kids 2
- Spy Kids 3-D: Game Over
- That's So Raven
- Totally Spies
- Transformers

COLLECT THEM ALL!

Now available wherever books are sold or at www.TOKYOPOP.com/shop

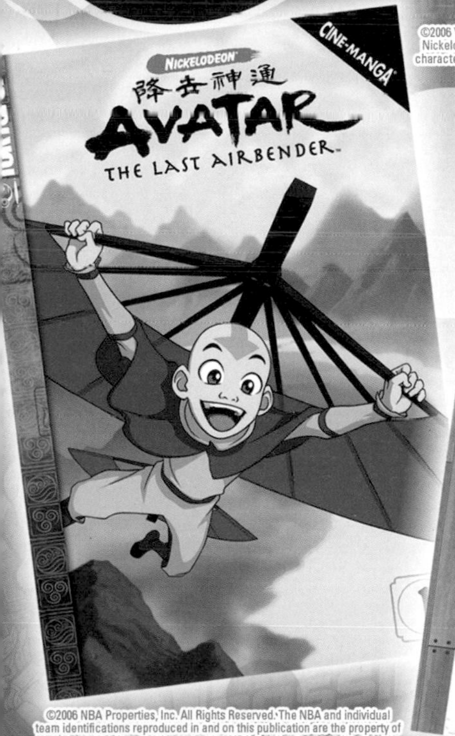
NICKELODEON
CINE-MANGA
AVATAR
THE LAST AIRBENDER

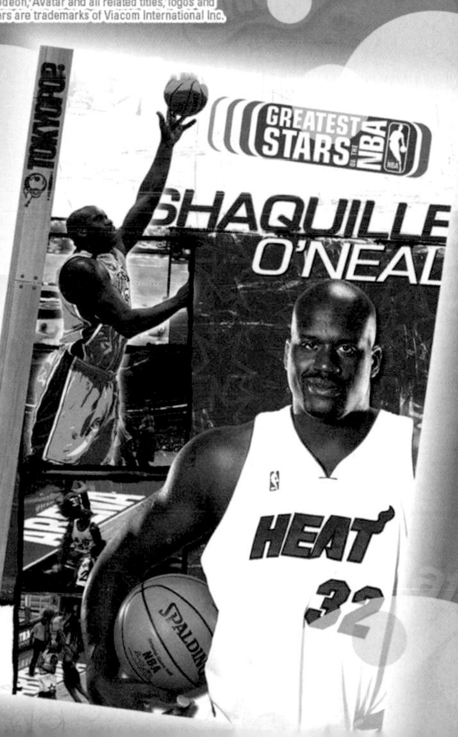
TOKYOPOP
GREATEST STARS OF THE NBA
SHAQUILLE O'NEAL
HEAT
32
SPALDING

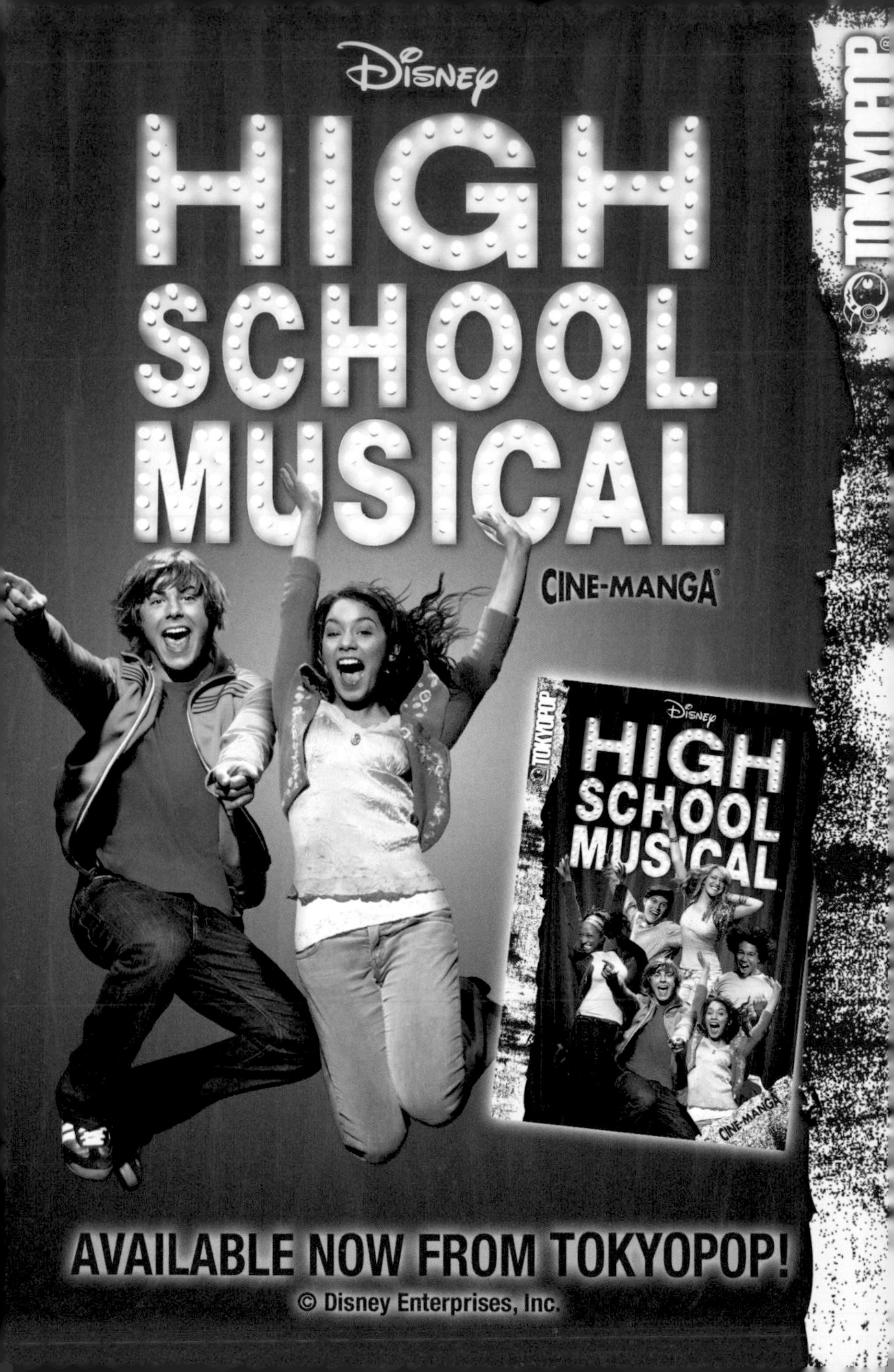

DISNEY
HIGH SCHOOL MUSICAL
CINE-MANGA
AVAILABLE NOW FROM TOKYOPOP!
© Disney Enterprises, Inc.
TOKYOPOP

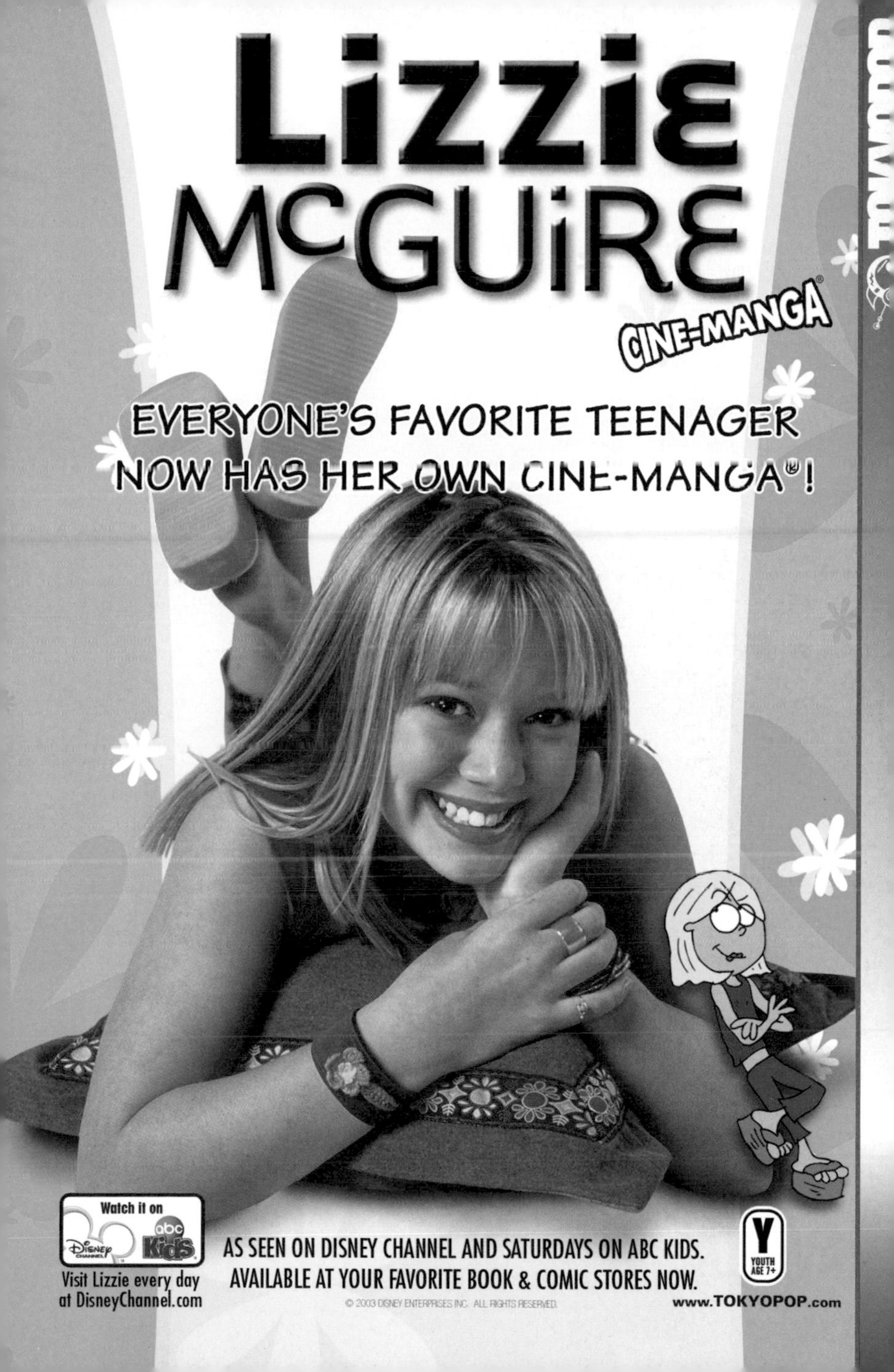
Lizzie McGUIRE
CINE-MANGA®
EVERYONE'S FAVORITE TEENAGER NOW HAS HER OWN CINE-MANGA®!
Watch it on Disney Channel abc Kids
Visit Lizzie every day at DisneyChannel.com
AS SEEN ON DISNEY CHANNEL AND SATURDAYS ON ABC KIDS.
AVAILABLE AT YOUR FAVORITE BOOK & COMIC STORES NOW.
© 2003 DISNEY ENTERPRISES INC. ALL RIGHTS RESERVED.
Y YOUTH AGE 7+
www.TOKYOPOP.com

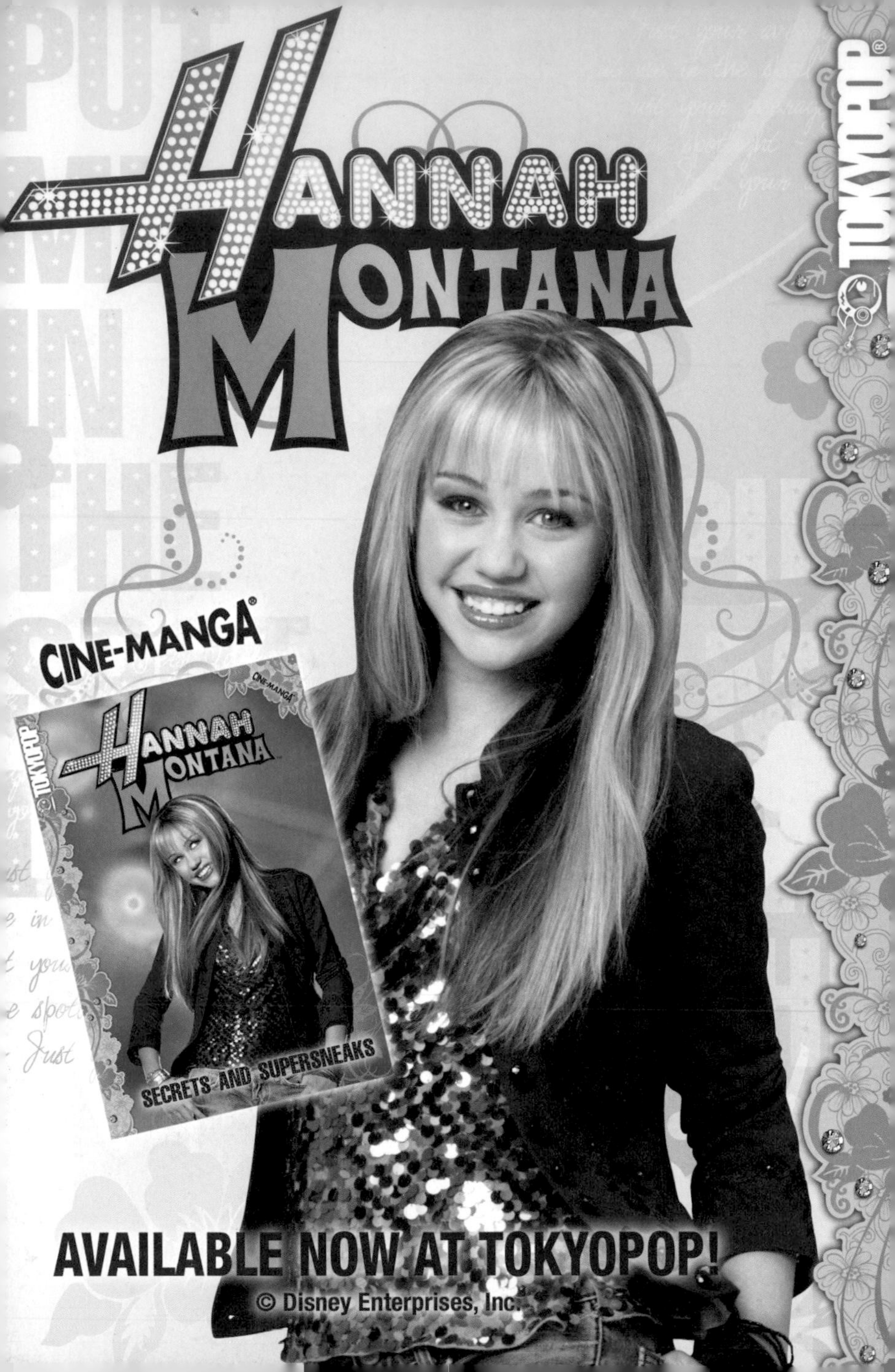
HANNAH MONTANA
TOKYOPOP®
CINE-MANGA®
CINE-MANGA®
HANNAH MONTANA
TOKYOPOP
SECRETS AND SUPERSNEAKS
AVAILABLE NOW AT TOKYOPOP!
© Disney Enterprises, Inc.

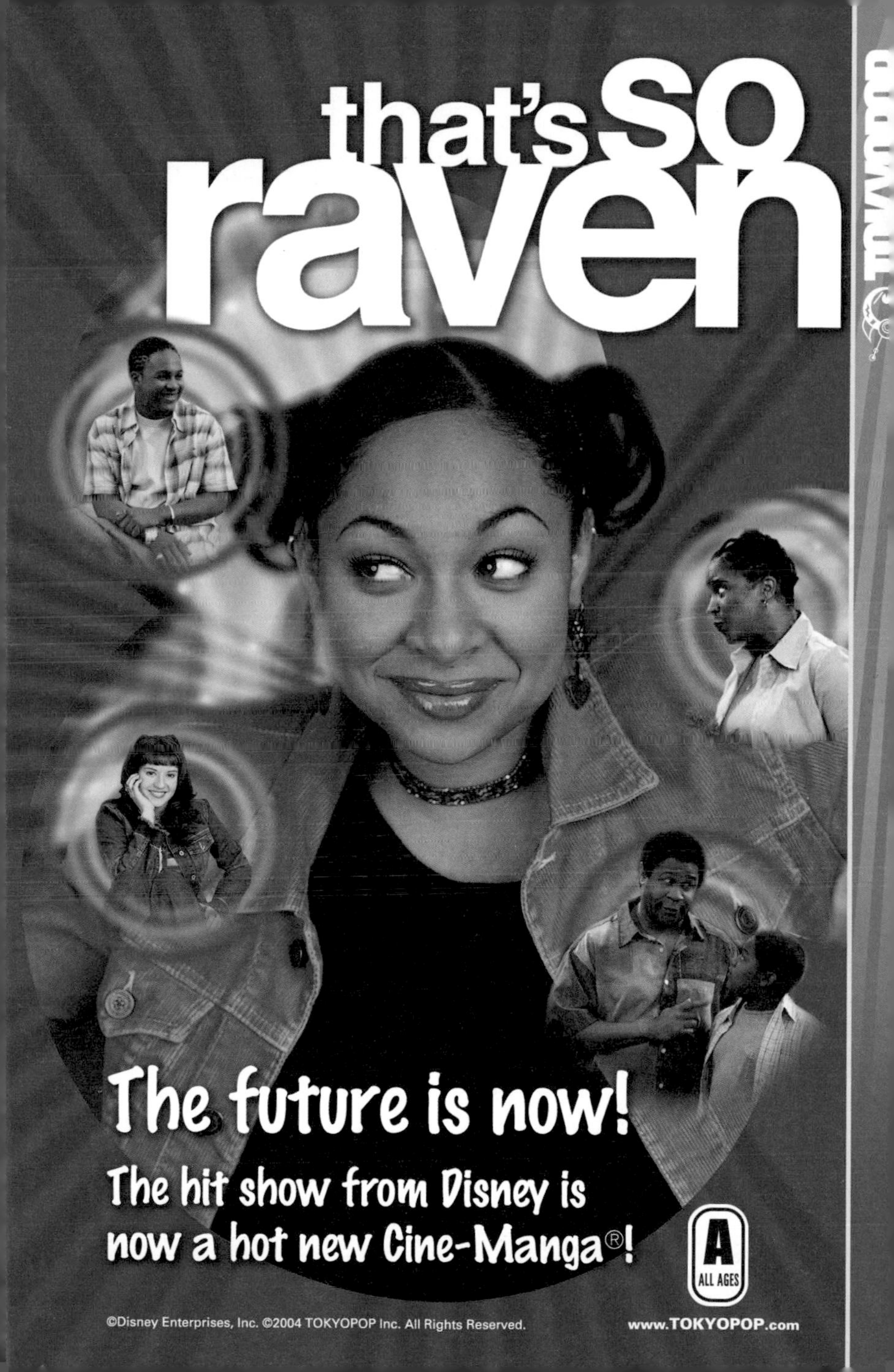

that's so raven
TOKYOPOP
The future is now!
The hit show from Disney is
now a hot new Cine-Manga®!
A
ALL AGES
©Disney Enterprises, Inc. ©2004 TOKYOPOP Inc. All Rights Reserved.
www.TOKYOPOP.com

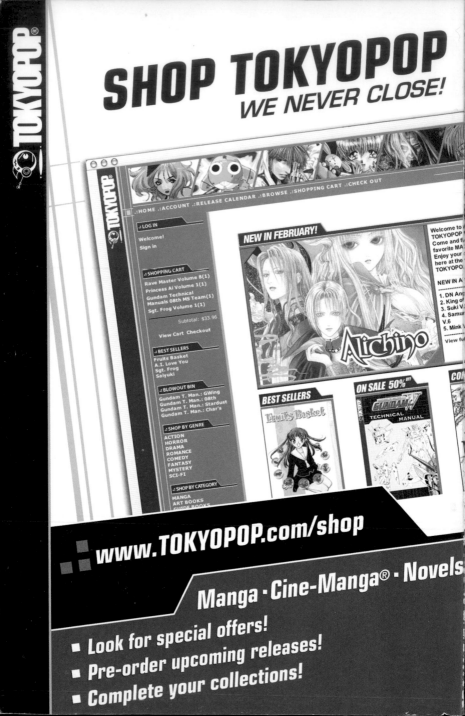